SPRING AND AUTUMN ANNALS

PRAISE FOR

Spring and Autumn Annals

"Written in the wake of her friend's suicide, *Spring and Autumn Annals* is a kind of epistolary diary: a chronicle driven by confusion, deliberation and grief. Like Christa Wolf's *One Day a Year*, *Annals* conveys the texture of time and the appearance of everyday objects in a disappeared world. The book is a treasure. Moving between the East Village, San Francisco, Topanga Canyon, and Stinson Beach with young children, di Prima's life is unbelievably rich. She studies Greek, writes, prepares dinners and feasts, and co-edits *Floating Bear* magazine. Diane di Prima is one of the greatest writers of her generation, and this book offers a window into its lives."

—Chris Kraus

"Extolled by a writer who radically devoted herself to the experiential truth of beauty and intellect, in poverty and grace, in independent dignity, and in the community of Beat consciousness, Diane Di Prima's *Spring and Autumn Annals* arrives as a long-lost charm of illuminated meditations to love, life, death, eros, and selflessness. An essential 1960s text of visionary rapaciousness."

—Thurston Moore

"Freddie Herko wished for a third love before he died; and what a love is in this book's beholding, saying, and release. Di Prima's dancing narrative, propelled and circling at the speed of thought, picking up every name and detailed perception as a rolling tide, fills me with gratitude for the truth of her eye. Nothing gets past it, not even the 'ballet slippers letting in the snow.'"

—**Ana Božičević**

"A masterpiece of literary reflection, as quest to archive her dancer friend's life, to make art at all costs, and the price dearly paid. Di Prima's observational capacity is profound, and her devotion and loyalty assures her deserved place as a national treasure. She generously instills in us the call of poetic remembrance as an act of resistance and gives voice to the marginalized participants in experimental cultural movements that carried courage in creative rebellion while envisioning freedom of the human spirit. Di Prima's poetic memoir of the artist journey is a triumph. A must read and reread for years to come."

—**Karen Finley**

spring and autumn annals

A CELEBRATION OF THE SEASONS FOR FREDDIE

Diane di Prima

City Lights Books | San Francisco

Cover photo by Peter Moore, "Portrait of Diane di Prima," May 22, 1964
© 2021 Barbara Moore / Licensed by VAGA at Artists Rights Society
(ARS), NY, Courtesy Paula Cooper Gallery, New York

Cover design by Gerilyn Attebery

ISBN: 978-0-87286-880-9
eISBN: 978-0-87286-857-1

Library of Congress Cataloging-in-Publication Data

Names: di Prima, Diane, 1934- author.
Title: Spring and autumn annals : a celebration of the seasons for freddie
    / Diane di Prima.
Description: San Francisco : City Lights Books, 2021. | Includes
    bibliographical references and index.
Identifiers: LCCN 2021009935 | ISBN 9780872868809 (paperback)
Subjects: LCSH: Di Prima, Diane. | Di Prima, Diane—Friends and
associates.
    | Poets, American—20th century—Biography.
Classification: LCC PS3507.I68 Z46 2018 | DDC 811/.54—dc23
LC record available at https://lccn.loc.gov/2021009935

Love and thanks to Ammiel Alcalay,
my favorite superhero who rides
deadlines like thunderbolts.
With thanks to Bret Rohmer
who worked with me over many
years on different forms of the text.

City Lights Books are published at the City Lights Bookstore
261 Columbus Avenue, San Francisco, CA 94133
www.citylights.com

*For Sheppard, who unraveled time
and went there with me 55 years later*

FOREWORD

BORN IN 1934, Diane di Prima was 30 years old when she began writing *Spring and Autumn Annals: A Celebration of the Seasons* in 1964. Her first poems had been published in 1950, at the age of 16, in New York City's Hunter High School literary magazine, *Argos*, along with those of classmate and lifelong friend Audre Lorde, whose first book di Prima would go on to publish in 1968 with Poets Press, a publishing venture she founded the same year she began writing *Annals*.

By 1953, di Prima had begun corresponding with poets Kenneth Patchen and Ezra Pound. In 1955, she went to visit Pound. Declared *non compos mentis* by a state that did not want to put him on trial for charges of treason, Pound was still incarcerated at St. Elizabeths Hospital for the Criminally Insane in Washington, DC, a building that now houses the Department of Homeland Security. Pound would remain a lifelong source, and she continued teaching his work, no matter how unfashionable it became. Her first book of poems, *This Kind of Bird*

Flies Backwards, came out in 1958, followed in 1961 by a book of short prose pieces, *Dinners and Nightmares*. That same year, along with then LeRoi Jones (Amiri Baraka), di Prima began publishing *The Floating Bear*, a mimeograph magazine that made it possible for writers who couldn't afford long-distance telephone calls or frequent travel to connect with each other and engage in the rapid dissemination of new work, a mode that, for one, Charles Olson—a central figure of the period— was most grateful to have available. In many ways, *The Bear* served as a bridge between the little magazines of the 1950s and early 1960s and the development of the underground press movement of the later 1960s when, through the auspices of Liberation News Service, a syndicated wire outfit based in New York, di Prima began freely disseminating each of her new "Revolutionary Letters" to radical newspapers from coast to coast.

It was also in 1961 that di Prima co-founded the New York Poets Theatre, an initiative central to the world depicted in *Annals*. First housed behind an art gallery in New York's East Village, the space, as di Prima describes it, "was a large, dark, back room with a stage and little else… the back room had minimal stage lighting and very little heat." Later it moved to St. Mark's Place and the New Bowery Theatre, "a real theater…with hanging sign, and a stoop, entry and lobby and seats and a proscenium stage." With its unique mix of poets, dancers, choreographers, visual artists, and musicians, the theatre performed works by a wide range of writers, including di Prima herself, Michael McClure, Robert Duncan, Frank O'Hara, John Wieners, and even Wallace Stevens. And a score that might be composed and performed by Cecil Taylor. While di Prima's foundational role in this crucial period of creating new vessels to push the limits of what had been available or possible has never been questioned, it has also hardly been examined in more than cursory ways, and *Annals* offers entry into this world in a most intimate and dramatic fashion.

While my discussions with Diane about *Annals* began in 2014, it is only at this remove that I have come to understand the emotional and historical weight that this book—in all its various projected forms—held for her. And why, despite her true enthusiasm for it to see the light of day, it may have still been hard for her to let go of. Sheppard Powell, Diane's husband and partner in all things, has emphasized that it was Diane's steadfast allegiance to this largely disappeared world, to all those who had given their all to partake in its wild extravagance, that made her want to transmit that whole realm through a version that would have included, at one point, perhaps hundreds of photographs.

Although a few excerpts of *Spring and Autumn Annals* have appeared over the years, this is its first full publication. Written after the death of di Prima's dear friend, the dancer, choreographer, and musician Fred Herko, an important figure in the burgeoning downtown New York scene of the late 1950s and early 1960s, it served as a way for di Prima to not just mourn her loss but also "hold still." As she wrote:

> *Freddie Herko died on October 27, 1964,*
> *and I wrote this as a letter to him for a year.*
> *Donald Allen once suggested that I should*
> *write something sometime with the organizing*
> *principle being the four seasons, since I seemed*
> *to think in those terms a lot.*

When Freddie died I was in shock. After a couple of days I began to go to my study in the afternoon, light a stick of incense, and write until it burned all the way down (about 40 minutes). The incense gave me a way to hold still for a certain amount of time and write. I type as fast as I can, without cleaning up mistakes, or spelling. Thought of it as a letter to Freddie. It stopped on October 27, 1965, a year to the day after he died. Some time after that I cleaned up the stream-of-consciousness and made something people could read.

When I asked about her earlier idea of a version of *Annals* that would be composed of text and photos, Diane responded: "In the year I wrote it, we lost the theatre, and the house on Cooper Square. All the theatre sets (now priceless), assemblages and a painting by George Herms for a McClure play, a statue by Peter Agostini, some parts of a Red Grooms set for a Kenward Elmslie play, *Guinevere, or the Death of a Kangaroo*, a drawing by George Grosz and a sketch on a restaurant napkin by Dali, etc., all of it went out on the sidewalk in boxes. I had called the Whitney Museum and asked if they wanted to come down and look at the stuff but, no thanks, they didn't. I finished *Spring and Autumn Annals* at the Broadway Central Hotel where we all lived in one large room with various cots for the kids. It seems to me that it was then that I knew that I wanted the pictures. A whole world had been swept away and I knew 'one picture worth a thousand words.'"

In the mid-1970s, along with painter, illustrator, designer, editor, and close friend Bret Rohmer, di Prima began putting together a mock-up of the book. At some point, there was a possibility that Frontier Press, run by Harvey Brown, a former student of Charles Olson's during Olson's few years of teaching at Buffalo, would publish it. Then it was slated to come out with Richard Grossinger at North Atlantic, but that never came to pass. While only a few of the photographs have been reproduced here, the present edition at least provides a glimmer into what that probably now impossible version might have looked like.

During the years we worked on corrections and corroborating several versions of the manuscript, I kept coming back to my initial reaction on first reading *Annals* and my growing sense of Diane's extraordinary achievement as a prose stylist. Given that her vision was formed at a time of an unprecedented range of unique approaches to prose by her contemporaries, all of whom she knew well—from Kerouac and Burroughs to Robert Creeley, Hubert Selby Jr., Ed Dorn, LeRoi Jones/Amiri Baraka, Michael Rumaker, and so many others—she was able to forge a style all her own. In interviews she often mentioned Gertrude Stein and Hemingway as sources. While that feels right, it isn't obvious, nor does it tell the whole story. One of her very great achievements is her absolute reliance on plain language that both encompasses and encloses her vast erudition and knowledge of mythological, religious, and alchemical systems, only hinted at or secretly disclosed through the narrative pace of sentence, syntax, and prose segment. Nowhere is this more evident than in *Annals*. While there is an enormous gap in prose works between *Dinners and Nightmares* (1961) and *Recollections of My Life as a Woman* (2001), there was a sense that *Recollections* might open up the space for exploring that gap, making it possible to publish *Annals* and other unpublished prose work from those years, and create the further basis for also thinking about di Prima as an important prose writer. But a cruel and belittling hit piece in the *New York Times*, clearly meant to put di Prima in her place—beyond the confines of "polite" society, unworthy of prolonged or even *any* attention—made that just so much harder. And it is only now, sadly but with great joy, that we finally have this masterpiece in hand.

The narrative of *Spring and Autumn Annals* ranges from 1954 to 1965, with several forays into di Prima's childhood memories of growing up in Brooklyn, 1954 being the year Herko and di Prima met, on a park bench. She was struck by Herko: "He was the first dancer I'd met who knew other arts, and knew them well....We soon had a language and viewpoint all our own. He was... closer than any lover, and remained so for ten years. We bonded rapidly and utterly." Still living with his parents in Ossining, New York, while attending the Julliard School in Manhattan, he was studying to be a pianist. Born in 1936, and only twenty-nine at the time of his death, Herko was a legend among his contemporaries. Nevertheless, it has taken a long time for his reputation as an innovative artist to be recognized, even though he was a founding member of the Judson Dance Theater and an early member of the Warhol Factory.

While some might have thought of his death as yet another performance, sailing out the fifth floor window of an apartment on Cornelia Street in Greenwich Village and landing on the sidewalk with Mozart's Coronation Mass on the record player, di Prima's depiction of the world they inhabited may seem counterintuitive to present readers unfamiliar with the density, velocity, and extraordinarily innovative accomplishments of the period. As this group of friends, some now famous, clung to each other for dear life, the world around them hurtled toward erasure and obliteration. While many names appear in *Spring and Autumn Annals*, some immediately familiar and others not, there are no hierarchies, no jockeying for position, an impulse that has become second nature in so many quarters in the present world of artistic careerism. Amid the chaos and struggle of attempting to live lives that hadn't quite yet been lived that way, what remains most striking is di Prima's understanding of the necessity to record and remember, to establish the actuality of a world operating under very different conditions, at the edge of other precipices. Though unseen for over fifty years, *Spring and Autumn Annals* bursts forth with unyielding clarity and the courage to at least offer permission, despite the cost.

AMMIEL ALCALAY

fall

Let us now call up the slow pace of those evenings. Fall. The Fall of the Year. The Fall of Mankind. Out of what energy, what anger, what high windows now? The persistent voice at the door "DiPrima, open the door. Hey, dipreeee!!!" And the cold hallway, unfolding the double doors, letting in Freddie and who? Whoever trailed with him thru the frostmarked airs. The letting in Freddie, and the hundred cups of coffee. The voice of complaint: I have another cold. I have another cough. My toe won't point. My back. My hair too long, too short. The Alan shaving. The Mini just to *her* feet, the Alex not yet turning over. The slow grey of the sky, wind over rooftops. The magic & evil fumes of our large gas heater. Huddled over it, one spot on my ass always burning. Finally tearing the cloth on my old blue jeans. The hundred thousand coffees in that stainless steel pot. Of which glass top now broken. One of the last things Freddie made, holes in that top. Hard now to replace it, glittering reproach. The Winter soups full of garlic. Sometimes a fire. The silence stiffens now in our high white halls. This fall had been filled with bongo drums and castanets. As the summer had been. I think now with something like remorse of a dirty grey platform, some kind of dolly, loading platform dragged from construction site, dragged into that same hall, that now freezing silence, and left by that mad fey creature. How angry I was! How I dragged it out again, cursing, saying I had just gotten the hallway clear. It sat in front of the house for a day or two. The creature returned, looked sad, and wanted to take it in again. He said he wanted to put it on the roof. He wanted to sit on it when he played his drums. And we said no, most vehemently, how we

3

were clearing the roof, had cleared the hall. We cleared the hail all right. We cleared the roof, too.

What I really can't take are the mornings without the sun. To rise in the bleak wind, as if we were rising on the edge of the North Sea. Iron in the sky and in my chest. Iron in the coffee. Taste of gnashing teeth. The clouds not even signaling to each other. Strong wind, and the tree not stirring, layer on layer of me meeting silence on silence. Creak of the washing machine, noises of Alex. Stands in for one Freddie hundreds of Bowery people. Visions of Kirby float over Ninth Avenue. So much won clear. But to have no sun, no yellow light at all. Only the greys, greyblues, at most the white, the underside of pigeons. Or the white ruff of the cat.

The grey velveteen lives again on the top of our trunk. Our trunk of theatre cloths, in the living room. Whence it had been snatched by Freddie, carried off. To be bartered for amphetamine or cocaine. Here in what he called the navel of the earth. Hub o' the universe, the lower east side. One more love he wanted, he told me, before he died. Told me it was Billy Gray, poor foolish Billy. Dragged to the roof a sofa, made a tent, the gypsy king, for loving Billy in. Who floated in, and floated out again. Hardly aware what hopes were pinned on him. Never aware at all.

Oh, Freddie, this is the first thing I could weep for. That your third love didn't come to you on Ridge Street. Didn't come, so far as we know, but do we know? Did no third love come to you, no trundling burst? Did the sugar cubes bring you at last no such secrets? Did you finally find all things reaching out and loving you, and you, did you not settle into this love, at peace, nestling, as Jeanne says "in the arms of Kali"? So that Billy and his secrets floated off painlessly, out of reach, so that Arione, Debbie, Kirby, George, the panorama of your three-ring circus, slipped further than arms-length from you, supporting and singing. I pray now that your third love came, in silver shoes, and veiled, that she glittered and danced for you, a boy-girl, a child with the secrets. That you followed *her out the window.*

And then the leaves fell. None would fall before. They all came down, they filled up Washington Square. They crunch in Tompkins Square under all our feet. When we dare to walk there, without you, at your side. Debbie in tears because she is still a novice. The old men sunning, and the children skating. Well, they will tear it up, thank god, and one more echo / will spread like ripples / out of reach at last.

So hard to sing hymns of joy in this iron air. And yet we know the age of gold returns. That you have bought it back for us. The king. Another gypsy king, that's all. Bartering blood for gold, to kill this grey. Blanketing. *Crépuscule du matin. Crépuscule de l'après-midi.* Interlocking shadows. The alchemy that turned this black to gold.

Fall to me used to mean new notebooks, crisp, unused erasers, box upon box of pencils. Bottles of ink. Plans, things to study, schedules for the evenings. Chrysanthemums, a flower I'd always hated. I've finally learned to love them. Will I learn to love trees now too? Taking on characteristics not my own. After a while, fall came to mean winter was coming. That was later, when clothes weren't warm enough, or there weren't enough of them to keep out wind. The ballet slippers letting in the snow. Walking on subway grates where the warm winds blow. winter on winter coming, all too long. All making colds, and fevers, and numb hands. That hurt when you got to a house, or to a bar. This kind of fall stood for apartment hunting, or going home if there was already a home. The digging in, books, wood, food, all kinds of work. Provisioning the house for the time ahead.

I remember the fall you came to live on Amsterdam Avenue. The long tunnel of a house we had acquired. Your slow process of leaving music, for the dance. Long process of *leaving* Ossining, for the city. Ambitious unrealized theatre, a piece called "The Project"; a magazine, still undone, then titled "Riff." Longley's, where coffee after the first cup was free. The Whitney Museum, with its small dumpy reading room. Green rug, soft chairs, HOW WARM IT WAS. How warm the library, across the street. Though the glass windows looking at the street made it not half so snug. The holy air in the Brancusi room, where I would go to pray. How often we met there. Later, but that was spring, we were betrothed there. All the lovely, luxurious bathrooms of those places. Warm they were, and clean, with toilet paper. Hot water to wash our hands. Our few, brave baths, at home. The slow tub in the kitchen, long hours spent filling it up. The green & greasy yellow of kitchen walls. The rickety stove, an early twenties model, with high oven heating the room. Beans always on it, or lentils, bag after bag of garbage. Which we had been instructed to throw thru the window. Into the house next door. "What'sa matter" the super would say, "you don't have a window? You put it in pails, then I gotta put the pails out." House next door had been empty for twenty-eight years. The bar on the ground floor still going. All kinds of people & rats still living upstairs.

I remember now the building you found this summer. On Attorney Street, how you took me to look at it. Abandoned; you thought you might just move in. But wanted to see if maybe, on the off-chance, I'd like it enough to try to make Alan buy it. (You always thought Alan & I were magic people, that we could do anything we wanted.) You tried to make Arione buy it, but she wanted another. It was a lovely building, very old. We tried to break into it, but couldn't make it. Stood across the street a long time, looking at it. Red brick it was, with blue-green around the windows. Blue-green doors, on a street that shouldn't have been there.

I think it was winter on Amsterdam Avenue by the time they broke the window. Not Fall at all. Was that the first fall I knew you? The one before that had been so desolate. My girl, the woman I loved, had gone back to college. To the same school we'd both left. Leaving me desolate in our old apartment. Piano, and ballet bar, there on East Fifth Street. No, I had known you then. Because, that Fall, on East Fifth Street, I took you home. And took a creature home who thought she loved you. A runaway skeleton, just sixteen years old. Who slept in our bed. Linda Brown was her name. A tiny, ferret-creature, who whined a lot.

7

So it was the summer of '54 I met you. Or the spring. Ten years ago. Sat down on a park bench beside you, in the rain. Took you from there to Rienzi's, for some coffee. You were fat-ish. Terribly pleased with yourself, you played the piano. Lived in Ossining. Where we went for a visit. Watched you swim, plump and narcissistic, in a pool. From there to your parents' sad, ranch-style Westchester house. Where you played the piano for us, as I had never heard the piano played. You were not brilliant, you were not there at all. The music was there, not you, not you at all. NO ONE WAS PLAYING, the music was simply coming into being. And this among wall-to-wall carpeting, silly green plants, silly sofas. That later, even sillier, got covered with white satin. So that no one could sit there at all, and the end tables were painted white and gilded on the mouldings. Antiqued.

That fall you must have started at Juilliard. That fall started you dancing. Learning to fly. In the slow grey light I rose, took class, played the piano. Worked for a few months in a physics lab. Found there only pigeons free, who had flown in. Everything, everyone else was "Classified." That fall, ten years ago, I almost died. Missing my woman and my long, blonde ,friend. Who had hitched to the other coast with a dyke named Brandy. I remember there was a bar called the Montmartre. Folksinging, and bongo drums. A hodge-podge. Serving its purpose by being dark & cool. So that you could hide, could drink, could sing or weep. The richness, the unendurable thickness of my life. Why I do not want to put that into the world. Why I keep claiming movies should be only movies. No sound. And all shows should be one-man shows. The thickness of things, cutting my way thru that.

8

At Montmartre, that fall, almost twenty, I wept a lot. Drinking double gins one after the other. Fucking a lot, then coming back to the bar. Weary all the time with the weight of a desolation. A bitterness in the throat. Now, ten years later, that weight has returned to me. A ripe fruit in the hand. To be destroyed, or eaten.

O'Meara came back to me that black November. Back to my house and bed, and we made love. That only once, and we kept house, kept Christmas. How bleak her lovemaking was, like the kiss of an orphan. We raised up monies for Lori, away at school. Her tuition unpaid, her glasses a little askew. Met her at Christmas, the edge of Swarthmore campus. Her brand new lovergirl, Nell Commager, was there with her. We gave Lori six hundred dollars, a fortune to us. And went away. Not even stopping to walk those lawns again. So frightened was she that we would be seen.

The Fall is the high place from which to begin the year. The city year starts in Fall, the Jews are right. Spring may start country years, start green things growing, but Fall, the first cold wind that strikes the city, makes all before it new. How we had that fall on Amsterdam, how chaste it was. Our flight had been to Boston, to escape a lover of O'Meara's. A mad boy, really mad with paranoia. Driven to madness by the FBI. He'd been left here, paperless at the age of fourteen, by his father, who had been recalled to Yugoslavia, by Tito, and who feared, not without reason, to bring his son back with him. And so, Mike, paperless, reported to no authorities, lived for a longish time on the West Coast, came east, all was cool till one day he was finally tracked down at a temp employment office. Beginning of chase. But chase was only part one of the difficulty, the rest of it was his most unreasoning love for Joan O'Meara. Which had led them both into terrible troubles that summer. Finally an abortion, and Joan wanted to leave him. Easier to conceive of than accomplish. For that Mike would burst into tears, tear his hair, fall at her feet, lock her in the house. Lose her suitcase. Threaten to kill her cat. Finally, Joan went and hid at the house of a mad mathematician named Boris (there were several Mad Mathematicians left in the world in those days), and I trotted off to Mike's in the company of several strong ex-lovers. Mike tore his hair, etc. I left with suitcase while he was out of the house. Met Joan as arranged under the George Washington Bridge, and we set out for Boston, for to visit some friends. Hitchiking all the way. Got stopped by police outside of Worcester. Examining our bags they found a pound of telephone slugs, and a list of all the gay bars in Boston, meticulously labeled at top "Gay Bars in Boston" (pulled from complete file of same). Ride to station. Much questioning, on accounta (they said) two sixteen-year-olds had run away from Albany. Me very EXASPERATED, on accounta having just acquired my majority. Finally, all cooled by a call to my family, who assured the cops (with tears) that we were twenty-one & therefore capable of getting to Boston. (Mother-reproach: "All Poets Are Hoboes"). Much fascination with telephone slugs. How did they work? Showed them. They kept the slugs, turned us loose.

But no more hitchhiking they said, get on a bus. How can we do that we asked, having two dollars between us. Don't know they said, but no more hitchhiking. We consulted together, conscience and heart, as to who might owe us a favor, wire us some money, and came up with Big Bruce, a large Black guy we had kept from suicide the Winter before, when he had been walking MacDougal Street with his wrists cut and his trench coat pockets full of blood. We called him collect at the socialist summer camp where he was working, his family lived in Worcester, and we made it there. Found dozens of folks in five rooms, good franks and spaghetti. "Line those stomachs, you two must be hungry." O'Meara played poker all night, lost to a twelve-year-old. I slept in a bed. With how many other people? People sleeping in armchairs, sleeping on floors. Fried fish in the air, and fried fish on the table. The questions "That boy Bruce OK? You sure he's not in jail or anything?" Slightly ashamed we were to take Bruce's money, where here it was more needed. A wire arrived in the morning for $25. We bought fruit and milk for the household, and set out.

So much more to this really, anyway got to Boston. And got chased, Mike having called my family who told where we were headed. Hiding out in Boston subways. Drinking vodka on the banks of the Charles. Keeping vigil one night in very proper Brookline apartment, with a heavy glass ashtray in one hand, waiting for that young man to break in.... Finally, left for home, O'Meara staying behind. HOME, Amsterdam Avenue, where we had just found our pad.

Home was there, but had been ransacked in our absence. The great door broken off its hinges, we put up

11

giant bolts, two by fours, across it, and never used it again. Built a bookcase across the front of it and came in thru the kitchen. I spent a day or two picking up the papers scattered by Mike's mad hands, in his search for us, for addresses and clues. Luckily had left the address file somewhere else, had hidden it before we both took off. September first, we took the house, this was September fifth or thereabouts. Not really Fall, but fall, in that special way that Fall comes to New York. The process of digging in before the winter. Preparation of the caves for hibernation.

The Cave, this pad, number 6 Amsterdam Avenue. Had belonged to Nicky Thacher. To whom we promised a fortune, one hundred dollars, in order to take it over. Paid him forty. Owe him sixty to this day. Hole in the floor in the front room, by the fireplace. "Dropped a burning log and forgot to pick it up" said Nicky. Stoned, always. Hole revealed underpinnings of house, broad solid beams, charred. Months later had it covered, made new by Mo. Kitchen in the back, then a small middle room. Where file drawer on top of dresser held all my writings. Large boxes filled with wood resided there always. Called it the woodshed, as in Mezz Mezzrow's book "woodshedding" meant staying home & practicing. What Sonny Rollins was doing on the Bridge. When we took possession the kitchen & the woodshed were both filled with shredded paper, the abode of rats. Much garbage left behind by Nicky & chick. Shredded & soft, for nests, we cleaned it out. Didn't think much about it. After woodshed, all in a row, this being a "railroad flat" came a slightly larger room with a bed, a drawing table, and a kerosene heater. Heater didn't work, and we threw it out. Drawing table is with me still, after many side trips and excursions to other houses. It is very beautiful, all marked and scarred with the lines of many razors and exacto knives and pens. Bed was a marvel that had no spring at all. A series of slats cut to fit inside the frame, and a very lumpy mattress on top of that. Then the large front room where the hole in the floor was. Held all our boxes, not much different from the ratgarbage in the back. Not much different after Mike had been thru them. There was a studio couch there, green, opened double in emergencies, which turned out to be nearly always. Two large front windows opened on Amsterdam Avenue. Across the street a Miles Shoe factory. Where nothing ever happened. Fire escape on which would shine the moon. But we didn't know that yet.

Mezz Mezzrow's book, *Really the Blues*, and another book, called *Flee the Angry Strangers*. Exquisite cover drawing, hard & beat. Delicate, tender ankle of chick on couch. Man with a horn. Have looked for that book since, but never found it. That was before, on Fifth Street. A magazine around then too, called *Climax*. Signals that other people out there somewhere were into the same scene. That's where we started.

After a while you would occupy that couch, but at first it was Bobi Schwartz. I would get up in the cold, my breath making frost. Pull on my clothes, and motorcycle jacket, and trundle out with the shopping cart after wood. Three loads or so a day would just about do it. I'd make the fire, and then I'd wake you up. Fried eggs balanced nicely in plates on all your stomachs. O'Meara slow to start, you were much better. Bobi went back to sleep with the plate on his chest. That cat jumped on it, clattered it to the floor. It broke, she ate the eggs. The days went by.

The days went by. I studied Greek, wrote every afternoon. Bret came and joined us. Ben Carruthers got added just before Winter. Later, we worked for Eddie Jaffe making drinks. You finally left Juilliard, started dancing. At Ballet Theatre every afternoon. O'Meara and I going over for beginner's class. Supper at Chock Full O'Nuts in the red uptown sunsets. Central Park coloring the air with green & haze. Picking up Bret at the Art Students' League in the evenings. Going home to fire & talk, or wandering. The park, the streets, sometimes we went to the movies. You loved O'Meara, we were robust and healthy. Bret drew our pictures there, before the fire.

Our Thanksgiving dinner, the shopping I did with Joan on Ninth Avenue. Those stalls at dusk, abundance of food, the chilly red light floating over the Hudson River. Oysters and filet mignon and even duck. Our shot at elegance. Three kinds of wine, soup, pastries, somehow sorrowful. All eaten with chilly hands, fingers always cold.

I remember you came in day after day from class. You put down your bag, you took the quilt off the bed. A large loud clumsy afghan I had made, and you wrapped yourself in it and sat almost IN the fire. O'Meara's shoes were always burned at the tips from the fire, too. She tried so hard to keep her toes unnumb. Bret and I were more robust, with stiff fingers. I typed mistakes from cold, he drew OK. Used poems and still lifes to keep the fire going.

14

Did that for two years, after estranging summer. You lost your fat, and began to be a dancer. Joan moved away, seeking always Madison Avenue. The second Fall I typed on a large poem. My Greek improved, we acquired a double bed. Which I moved underneath those great front windows. By then the floor was fixed. Moon shone right in. I shared the double bed with Bret, and others. We waited for the first snow to start screwing. A kind of ritual, unversed as we were. Six men with keys came and went, I was more skilled than I had been at making fires. I had a diaphragm. Whoever came now brought wood, ate soup. A fair exchange. The bed in the inner room was practically yours. Then you moved out, to Prince Street, with Eddie Johnson

That second Fall found me trying to hold still. I asked you if you wanted to have a baby. You hooted. Marcia Dale visited us a lot. With her long flat hair, theosophy, and wheat germ. Enlightened Marcia. One of her cookies fed ten men for a week. Raisins & soy & whatnot. Young Mike, Mike Wieners, not to be confused with Dirty Mike. Or Little Mike, who had been O'Meara's lover. Terrible paintings, but he was sixteen years old. Everyone swore Mike was a terrible genius. And Big Mike. And another one, went finally to bed with a wet oil painting. At which point we all gave up on him.

How fastidious you were in the midst of all this. You and Joan like two children still aftaid to get dirty. Sat and looked on together, weeping a little. How could we tell you that it was really OK? We tried, sometimes. You've often reminded me since of one afternoon. It was November, the sun was streaming in, the house felt so clean tho it was not, the kind of clean, that a place gets with soot, and being swept often and never washed. I was sitting in front of the fire, in my jeans and white sweatshirt, the costume I wore all Winter, and still do. I sat with my back to the door, the kitchen entrance. I had a block of old white plaster of paris. Long wet and dried and hard, and I was carving it. With a screwdriver and a hammer was carving it. White dust in the air, white light, clean coldness & fire. You told me often of the light of that moment. You swung your key round, you walked in, there was music.

Fall is nesting time always, a giant separate anger. Based on the will to survive, to stay warm and moving. In '55 moved to Amsterdam Avenue. In '56 bedded down for another year. Our friendship with Frenchie, large, doleful & European. "What" he enquired on meeting "is your philosophy?" I grunted at him, I was making up your bed. "Mine" he said "is the philosophy of resigned desperation." Nicest existentialist I ever met. Like having a psychotic Saint Bernard.

Ben Carruthers was more like a catatonic poodle. Intelligent, shy, and given to quivering lithely. Beating out on the wall of the fireplace drumroll on drumroll. Sleeping with Joan O'Meara reluctantly. The studio couch of that first year, drawn up to the fire, served us all when the weather broke, as it finally did. Four or five of us piled into it, and slept in a heap. The two on the ends were coldest, and got up early.

Where were your questions, those small clouds on our ceiling? I hardly noticed them, I was so robust. I chased you around, demanding you eat "green and leafys." Telling you no one fastidious ever survived.

It finally got too cold for walks in the park. A brisk trot to the library was best. We heard that they were preparing to tear down Longley's. I wrote to Ezra Pound sometime that Fall.

The light uptown and down are not alike. Fall air up there, always seemed to be at twilight. Always red and distant, as it had been in my childhood behind the steeple of St. Stephen's Church in Brooklyn. There, and in Brooklyn, the sense of the water nearby. Perhaps it was the water made that air. Dull red sunsets like they used to be so fond of on Christmas cards. The kind of card my father sent all his clients, five hundred cards went out engraved with our names. Never a written word on any of them.

Downtown fall air is high, it rings of crystal. The Chrysler Building stands up in it. There are towers. It is, as Alan says, City of the Sun. Not so uptown. Up there till the wind got too cold they fished in the river. Caught eels, and they ate pigeons, I'm sure of it. Would often see a man walk home, one pigeon held carefully in his hand, a surreptitious swing to his cracking boots. Nevertheless it was hard to come down again.

Up there I was on an island, island air surrounded me. I dreamed at night of boats, as I did in Brooklyn. COULD HEAR FOG HORNS, often. Wharves were not far away, smokestacks faced outward, the river flowed to the sea.

Next Fall I found myself well launched on my life. As you were launched on yours. My belly big. My things piled up again, in dozens of boxes. Another downtown pad to clean, to paint. I dreamed of the walls uptown, the well-drawn faces. Graffiti. The Unicorns Shall Inherit the Earth.

The day you died, I drove thru Central Park with Audre who had come to pick me up, to take me out of that house where your women were crying, so that I could come to terms somehow with the deed. We entered the park, there had been a fire, it had been so dry this fall, this summer too. The smell of the burning leaves, and of the dry leaves rotting on damp earth. A sharp, sharp smell, acrid high in the nostrils. The smell of the leaves on the path at Swarthmore, the first fall that I ever lived in the country. What college was to me, was merely country. I had seen country summer before, but never its fall or spring. And found it astonishing, chiefly for its smell. That smell in the park that night somehow closed the circle, cut me loose. A cycle was finished, a whole Odyssey. We drove to the parking lot and sat there a little. So pointless, aimless like dead-end streets in San Francisco. Or the parking lot at the Cloisters in the spring, when Stefan picked me up and we drove there with Jeanne. He sat there, meeting his daughter, and I nursed her. The leaves, I come back to them, and the smell of wood fires. One circle after another closes around me. Concentric, some smaller, some larger, from one parking lot to another, from leaves to leaves, and the rain in the fireplace, wet woodsmoke and ashes. The cat smell too when the ashes cool off and she shits there.

It has all drawn gracefully to its natural conclusions. Like major chords at the end of a Mozart piece. I must set out, this cycle has come to its end. We sat last night in the movies looking at faces on the screen. Tartars, Mongolians, the peoples of Russia, taking our tent, or our bus-and-truck tour across Asia. We are being metamorphosed into you. Are becoming wanderers. I long for one more child before we go. Wonder if I'll have time. Figure it out. To travel all day, and be at home at night, requires that while you travel you take your rest. Letting the other one drive, he rests while you set up a house. Tent, or station wagon, or even in a motel. Set out the home things, eat and write, write letters. It will all be possible, I shall not look back. We buried you under the wind, the seeds were blowing.

The circus wagon creaks, we cross the plains.

I remember that one Fall that you lived with Alan, the grace and bustle of that time. The morning on Houston Street when Jeanne looked up to see honey dripping down, down from the ceiling, down along our steam pipe. And went upstairs to find Alan had thrown a jar of honey at you. How astonished she was. I was not much less astonished. The gradual growing of holes in the walls, smashing of telephones, chairs, the breaking of windows. Not all of it in anger, sometimes Alan would just try to open a window. And it would give in his hand. How brave you were, we all thought, to live with him. Off Bowery Gallery opened that fall, and we took over the small back room for plays. You and Alan took it over. I moved away to the safety and space of East Fourth Street. The McClures having given out after

19

two Fall months there. Why? we often wondered. Could Kyra not take the constant buffoonery? The walks Mike took with Bruce Conner & Ray Johnson. The bottles of ink thrown for paintings at empty billboards. The movies in Russian, the frankfurters at Grant's. She thought too many times of Baker's Beach. She saw unclearly and little the rooms she lived in. So they took off again, and I moved in to Fourth Street.

You took my old apartment to add to your own. And Alan made an office there, a rather mad office, stuffy with stuffed leather chairs, of use to no one. Except it gave him quiet, and I suspect gave you quiet. You were both painting a lot. We did the plays. Off Bowery Gallery cold, the walls a dreadful pink and black. The stage minute. Joanna Vischer bitching. Rehearsals late. Jerry Benjamin hysterical. You madly typing stencils, mailing flyers. Working so hard and arguing so much, you must have been very happy. I remember rehearsing *Discontent* with you, and Alan throwing an armload of costumes and props and you ducking and me being in the line of fire. And vowing I'd never do anything with either of you again. One of those pointless vows made in desperation. You did the plays and a second set of plays. Typed rehearsal schedules, answered telephones. Activities so unlike you I wonder at them. Activities so unlike me, I'm doing them still. On Sunday night, two nights before you died, I dreamed of a kindly man admonishing me, telling me not to do those theatre things. That my business was to write, leave the rest alone. It would take care of itself. The dream went on, the people turned into you, I forgot the rest. But woke in tears, and sobbing.

Sobbed till dawn. In the morning woke, you called, you told me you'd killed the children. "All the children in the world."

So we played *Discontent of the Russian Prince* together. Then you went on to play it with someone else. That was a good Fall, Ann Holt, so pale she was hardly there at all. So thin and cold. Roi, the back of his head every night while he watched his play. Craned forward, like a bird, the ears aloft. Motionless, like some animal in the dark.

I carried Mini, which no one appreciated. I cried a lot in your kitchen, yours and Alan's. I thought you were mad to take on so pompous a man. A stiff. Not seeing yet the light, and the clumsy goodness. Before I left Houston Street there was that bust. The pounding on the door by the FBI. *The Floating Bear* scores, and we are finger-printed, Roi and I. Guaranteed to patch up a quarrel. Mini grew. Alan that morning, with the fuzz at the door, talking to Jeanne calmly, she was so frightened. Telling her that I had to go and explain things to some very stupid men who didn't like a story we had printed. She sat there silent with her eyes so big, neither you nor I had noticed her at all. Our first unending taste of law and courts. Later Alan wanting me to talk to the fuzz about my pad on Houston Street, when I had left it and he had moved in. The mad mad stories the two of you made up about it. How it was still my house, you hadn't sublet it, I had left Freddie, and he was mad with grief. And I thought Alan was mad, no one *talks* to cops. Still don't. One stays out of the way and hopes they'll leave. Thought you'd certainly come to no good, living with that madman.

The second madman, third love, never came to you. The first had been cruder, less cruel perhaps, a Saggitarius. Wanting to screw a lot, and everyone. Your chief bone of contention.

The day I passed you in the hallway, on Houston Street. You had come, so brave, with a suitcase, to stay with me. Till "The Baby" was born. In that house, with one cot, one sleeping bag, you settled, every word you said making jarring shapes in the air. All your misgivings. How I might die in childbirh. How I might be wrong about who the father was. Till I yelled and screamed, and finally spoke not at all. Very big, went out to work. That evening, coming back in October twilight, I passed you on the stair-case. Light thru the frosted glass of those big slum windows. That hall so much like the halls of my high school. Antiseptic, tiled, and chilly. How you said, you thought it would be better if you went. And I said yes. Brave suitcase in your hand, you went back to Vincent's. Where you lived, both of you, in a nest of incredible smells. Black sheets, reluctant bathtub, strange three-burner stove. A nest which Vincent has now made beautiful, and filled with paintings. But in those days I remember that I came there one night to sleep (for that, full of misgivings of my own, I didn't like to sleep alone at Houston Street) and went to the living room couch and turned back the cover, and many, many roaches scurried away, further into the bed, bed's grease and grey-black sheets.

How you came to see me in the hospital, some days after Jeanne's birth, wearing a suit and tie. Did you only have

22

one suit? I remember always the same one, incredibly awkward. The suit that's in those pictures we took on the boat, the day that Peter Hartman left for Europe. A kind of nondescript grey thing, that never fitted, that tried with some chagrin to disguise your faun shape. You were never built quite like a human being. Haunches, not hips.

This morning went to Coscia's, they had brioches, from Sutter's, and the rush of that Peter-farewell came back to me. The breakfast party: champagne and brioches. The web and flare of our lives. You and Peter. Peter and me. Roi. How we drank together, Anna officiating. The little girls Jeanne and Rosemarie getting high. Your high-handed skepticism.

Last night, for the first time in two weeks I dreamed of you. You came to some large arena, the edge of the stage, some kind of precipice into which you were going to leap. Out of doors. Our friends were gathered. You got ready to dance, the light was glorious. I held you in my arms as we stood together, held onto you for a long time, quite some time. Looked finally surreptitiously at the clock, and it read six fifteen. I knew I had held on long enough, that you wouldn't leap, that the time for that leap had come and passed. I knew you weren't going to have to die. Your death had been a bad dream I had dreamed. My dream seemed like the awakening out of a nightmare. YOU HAVE REVERSED THE PROCESS OF SLEEPING AND WAKING.

Never again will it be the same for me.

23

I take Jimmy's class, it is quite good and good for me, it is not your class at all, a different thing, but I do take it and yes, I do learn a lot. A lot from it. I am trying in some kind of way to plan Thanksgiving. There are three pumpkins downstairs, I feel that this is a start. Some kind of start. Venison stew, in wine? I see the gathering, I see last year's gathering, me trying to fend you off as you ate all the roast suckling pig, and other people, I said, who haven't come yet. First come first served you said, ducking under my arm. First come served once, I said, or maybe twice. Leave some for the others.

And now Jimmy is going to Holland in March to make dances, and we are having a theatre built for us, you see, if you had only held out, waited a little. We barely had time to tell you the apocalypse had happened, had already happened, that we were all in the clear. Told you that barely twenty-four hours before you died. If you had held out, but then, would we, any of us at all, would we have made it? Is it not your leap that is sending Jimmy to Europe, Alan to Kiesler, who'll help him build a theatre, send me back to the words that wait for me always? So faithful they are, the words, and they heal, somewhat. Not as cyanide would, but they do heal.

The new age, LA LUMIÉRE DE L'AURORE, is before us, Olson says that Mao says. But neither of them can picture the color of that. As, for instance, on achieving Nirvana, one is not (repeat: NOT) annihilated. Or, the description that Keats makes of autumn fields: "Really, without joking, chaste weather—Dian skies. I never liked stubble fields so much as now—Aye, better than the chilly green of spring." One becomes a large & glorious being. I thank you for the gift of two days. The drive to Westchester for your funeral. The skies pale blue, the stubble fields, the dried grasses, bright red trees. The Hudson from high ground in the dark. Stars blowing overhead. The cleanness of that cold air. Your bright, pinched smile in the coffin, master this. Make sense of it, di Prima, go ahead. Always organizing, always bustling about. Di Prima will know what to do about this. How to set it right. Mocking a little. Your father coming up to cover your hands. Because they were swollen, both broken at the wrists. The complete consummation, perfection of the sacrifice. Your brother enumerated the parts of it: your broken hips and ankles, wrists and thighs. The symmetry and wholeness of your flight. The calm (beatitude) with which you landed.

Alan and I plan lives, a game. "Send China a million cows" says Emperor Marlowe "and tell them it's a present." We sit back, we wait and see what China will send us. Our play Apocalypse: How We Will Live in Caves. Hoard Matches Now. Plan monasteries in Scotland, in Pennsylvania. I'm taking the train to London for a week, I have to buy some books, order paper for the press and thread for the looms, says Countess Diane taking up her walking stick. Meanwhile the plans nearer home: notebooks full of theatres. If you had waited you could have had your choice.

The Fall of the year that Jeanne was one year old. Our lives together, this time on Houston Street. How many times you came home terribly drunk. How you wished that Jeanne was your baby, I your mistress. I wrote *Necrophilia* for you, and waited. We shared a bed. Most nights you slept in my arms. My turn it was to mock a little, gently. I'm here, I told you, and if you want me take me. Anna sent us soup and stuffed cabbage, across the clothesline.

The following fall, when Zella had already left me. You moved upstairs, we had one of those Thanksgivings. I helped you move your stuff, to settle in. Your kitchen cupboard had one large corner missing, where Pauli had thrown an ax at Mo. Foreshadowing you and Alan.

Must make this Thanksgiving work somehow by making it different. By making it something else. There must be no echoes, no mirror-into-mirror. Help me.

When I brought Jeanne home from the hospital Mo came with me. I settled into the farthest room of my house. My trap-shaped apartment. Shaped like a meager L. Into the farthest corner of it, in fear. That the neighbors would by their hate kill the child and me. Fear of hunger, lack of warmth, half-painted rooms. Pink slum color showing thru the one coat of white. The cheapest white, $1.47 a gallon. Mo hung out the diapers, a face appeared at the window. Window next door, a hearty booming voice. Asked, is it a boy or a girl. Joyful and pleased. A girl Mo said. I'm glad said the voice I'm not the only one who'll be hanging out diapers. In she went, shutting her window. So we met Anna.

Anna, who came with us to your wake, who drove us to your wake. So that we could see the light in your face, no horror, the lack of confusion. We circled your house two or three times in the car, not able to find the funeral home, knowing you should have been there in the house, in that foolish white and gold living room with the piano. Or in the bedroom, a lawn spread away outside. But when we found the place it was a good place. A large white house. We walked inside, into the chilly night. The dead of other people in other rooms. But a high point of land and below the river. A large number of stars. I stopped in the outer room, took handfuls of prayer cards for the undead back home. Thinking how we lived in a fetishist society. Waiting to go in and see that which was you. They claimed was you. The undertaker very nervous sent everyone out and worked on the body a little. Like a portrait painter completing a difficult study. Proud of the job he'd done. Your brother telling us what a mess you'd been. When he came to identify you at the morgue. Don't think you'd liked the morgue. Proud undertaker then throwing open the doors (this is a part of autumn every year now). You not recognizable at first, then terribly recognizable. Almost dead. Smiling a little, terribly pleased with yourself. That I couldn't cry there, with your stoic family. I saw that white bouquet in the shape of a piano. With the white and black keys, and two notes on top. The irony of that. I knelt beside you. To pray to you, not God, all I could say was "don't be afraid Freddie, don't be afraid." I sat down. You heard me. Anna was crying. "And the scum of the earth still lives" said Anna. Alan took me outside. The stars were very white, there was Sirius, flashing. The river below, I cried to the freezing ground. To the wind, I was part of the wind, why it wails so much / is it's filled with the wailing of women around the earth.

Now dry-eyed I wonder where we will emerge. Angkor Wat. Benares. London. I am buying the offset press.

Your father told Alan how much your piano had cost him. Your sister-in-law told me what you had done with your room. Last time you were up there. You put out the furniture. Threw the mattress on the floor, lined the walls with mirrors. Unpacked innumerable beautiful boxes and little things. Pieces of cloth. "I don't know where they all came from." Lit candles, lay down on your mattress, gypsy king, and went to sleep for a week.

Drive back again next day, Alan a pallbearer. Bret talking a lot, keeping the fact at bay. The glory of the sun, the bright Fall. The turning leaves I'd never have gotten to see. Except you flew. I wore the cape, I thought you would like that, my black velvet cape to the floor wrapped me about, and I walked into the room where you lay when they all left. No one said me nay. I kissed you on the lips, and you were dead. You hadn't been dead yesterday when I touched your hand. Stiff lips, like wax, and cold; bristles of hair stiff too. I pressed Debbie's ring into your hand, for her sake, not yours. Heard you half-annoyed, bemused "Di Prima! You know where that's at." Told you yes, I knew, but it was only courtesy to take it, and it won't hurt you. They closed you in. Kept hearing *The Blossom*: "Oh, you are dead." Looked down at green hedges, saw flesh growing everywhere. Sprouting out of the ground.

December 13, 1964. Fifty days since you began your Bardo. I get up from the desk and count them again. To make sure. Fifty days. No, fifty days comes after the eclipse of the moon. The nineteenth. Forty-four days today. How long it seems. Counting days, on the red and white Gestetner calendar, finger touching each day

28

as I count them carefully off, like a process of freedom, lighter and lighter I get, I see they have passed. I see they have somehow passed. The sense of time this fall is somehow off. The sense of where we are. How the seasons change. And when. Do they change, does winter come with the first snow? No, winter still comes at the solstice, *sol invictus* returning in full brightness to the earth. The rest of this is different kinds of fall. As today for instance, driving thru mist, back from Millbrook, New York, in mist so thick that only the closest trees could be seen at all, and they were in mist. Thru that country you gave us this year by dying. Upstate New York. Sending us out there first in the clear October air, so that we return again and again now in mist. The closest trees are a black silhouette, the rest is smokiness, it comes and goes. "Anything could live in those woods" I say to Alan. He thinks of satyrs and naked maidens running across the road. I see mournful unshapely beestes, Blackwood creatures. Machen, Lovecraft, I hear witches' Sabbaths. No special joy, satyrs belong to the south, they are unmysterious.

Your wallet is lying on my desk. Mysterious. Yes. It has in it the feel of your skin, I wonder how it got there. How it got out of the Freddie box on the floor. Where it will go from here. The incense burns slowly, I have vowed to write of this till the incense stops burning.

Went yesterday to Millbrook, to a wedding. Timothy Leary one of the tribal chiefs, married a northern princess. The church was bare, was austere, no one played Bach. The Scandinavian princess, and the man, half-Celt, half-Pict, both required a Druid marriage, under

29

trees. It seemed as if the Romans had conquered Briton. Christianity had come, this makeshift church had just gone up, and out of compulsion, or out of courtesy, to those most sad and lonely conquerors, they married under its roof. An elegant token. The kind of thing they would do.

There were great festivities afterwards, and drink. The world was a forties movie. Headlights moved mysteriously in the fog. Up to and past the curve of the drawing room windows. Barbara Stanwyck floated in & out, her hair on fire. The princess, like all good Scandinavian women, looked to the fires with her little sister. That warmth should continue. Her mother oversaw, looked to the feast, the whole smoked fish, the endless heads of cheese, a white dog under her arm, her brocade gown floating behind her. I lay in bed upstairs, for I was sick. In a room you might have made. All hung with cloths. With Indian bedspreads on the walls and ceiling, and fur on the bed. A gypsy tent indeed. Belonging to one, Annette Peacock, beloved of Kirby. Alan says that you & she are of the same tribe. Well, brother, do you sleep? I tell you these stories, listen for your tread. You are not here today, the house is empty. Perhaps you have come to a womb door. I try not to push you on, or hold you back. In the book I pray for your enlightenment and release. But cannot picture it. There is another life for you and me. For all of us. Another life, at least. The proof is, that I'm almost glad of it.

This of the seasons changing puzzles me so. In the last two weeks I saw it become winter. It snowed at Millbrook, the great old oak was white, the woods were

silver, they gleamed like the diamond trees in *Grimms'*
Fairy Tales. And it became spring in New York a few
days later. Mist, and warmth, that softness of the air,
and yet I know it's fall, that winter will come at the
solstice. This is a week to beware of and rejoice in.
Eclipse comes the day before the moon is full. So that
not quite hits on that. And then, the solstice two days
after the full moon. An almost eclipse of the full moon
solstice. An almost. How time is awry. I cannot count
them anymore, the days. Just hope they somehow pass.
They somehow pass.

This fall this wedding showed us again our wedding.
Alan and I. Whom you gave to each other. That fall,
the sea like a third grown-up in the house. Keeping the
children in hand, and making the shape of our days
the sea, the mists on the long road from Stinson Beach,
that wound above the sea to San Francisco. The gulls,
the baby sharks dead on the sand. Pelicans, even egrets,
auguring well. The smiling face of Suzuki chanting the
sutra. The silence of our wedding ceremony. There
were no words. I bowed to him many times, and to
Suzuki, and to Buddha. The incense glowed. *Freddie*
Alan and I were married today read the telegram
I sent. There were no words, he bowed to me many
times. We returned to a barren house, almost no food.
Ate Lipton soup, packed our things, for the setting out.
Chilly and tired and hungry, for the first time free. Set
free in that damp air.

We set out down the coast with our pots and pans.
Two LaMontes in the back seat. Arrived in putrid air
in a purple dawn. Los Angeles, one star burned over

31

a mountain. Like the descent into hell. I wept in the car. For the first time saw streets I would gladly have bombed. Neat squares of lawn bought by the square foot. Set down in front of the shacks with plastic floors.

In Los Angeles there was no fall. Drove back to New York and into dirty snow. Saw you, but briefly, everyone was so angry. We had so many things we had to pack. Spent the solstice that year somewhere in western Texas.

And the first snow at Millbrook, two weeks ago, showed me again the first snow in '56. Which Bret & I waited for, before we made love. A strange kind of semi-celibacy, a rite. I don't remember if we screwed when the snow came. I only remember the waiting. And how strange it was, that it didn't snow in November, not at all. As it has not, here, this year. Only in the country, only north of here. We drove back last Monday thru a sparkling world. Which gradually faded just north of the city. The city untouched and matter-of-fact as ever.

There is no smell of Christmas here this year. No crowds, no lights, no music, no bright bundles. No children talking about Santa Claus. Greyness, a bleakness nothing can penetrate. And *sol invictus* rising thru that again. The world he returns to grinding to a stop. "Be not sad" says the *I Ching*. "Be like the sun at midday." Well, we try. When it finally fell, that year at Amsterdam Avenue, the fire escape became bars of glittering white. The moon shone on them, shone in thru the window. Shone all over the bed. The fire glowed. There were colors unnamable, and a great joy.

32

It is interesting how the seasons flicker before they change. One can always smell the season just ahead. And sometimes the one beyond that. It first turns to spring for me in January. It goes again, comes and goes, then comes to stay. But when it comes to stay, it turns to summer. The first fall winds, I smell the beginning of August. But they are fall winds, yearly, nevertheless. So we count off the years, so they pass, while we wait for a change. For the sun to come out and give the lie to that bleakness. For the lights to go on. Well, we won't wait too much longer, we'll make the sun, a generator, something, whatever we need. We'll build the Temple of Shiva in New York. That ought to change it somehow.

It was Fall that Mike Strong came to stay with me, on Fifth Street, and he had a strange disease. Red bumps came out on his groin, and under his arms. He was delirious, we slept in one bed. Three or four of us, don't know how many, sent for no doctors. Doctors were something we had never dreamed of. I told him he had bubonic plague, he laughed. Unmirthfully. I gave him sleeping pills because he was so delirious and keeping the rest of us awake. Finally one day he woke up lucid, and said "I think if I read Baudelaire today I'll vomit." I went out. Came back and he was better. He said " I read Baudelaire and I vomited." So it comes, the bubonic plague is a form of possession.

I think of all the seasons, fall is the longest. Slipping as it does from September to December. The changes in those months. September crystal skies, New York the sun city, the big apple. The bongo drums, amphetamine, the chatter. Classes at John McDowell's, constant bitching. The slow coming to life of Alan Marlowe. Who hibernates all summer. Then October, sun even brighter, cold coming into the air. The sudden endless smogs, settling in for a week at a time, blood-colored somehow, "smoky light." The day you jumped. The four days after, till we laid you in the earth. The sounds of the blowing seeds like the sounds of the sea. Glittering orange and gold, and the sultry earth. November. The purples, the smoky blues, the greys and browns. The trees now bare, their tops making endless purples. The hills in mist. The hills covered with snow. First frosts. Thanksgiving dinner, the old house filling again, rejoicing to itself. Fires and candles. The table opening to its full length. Performing, as seldom, its function. Full platters, dancing children.

I remember chasing you last year from the turkey, or was it pig, you and John Worden, who had come for thirds, while others were arriving. There being a shortage of meat, I chased you away. And so, this year bought enough, and more than enough. Refrigerator for weeks after possessed of a turkey demon. Bundles of stuffing that sat on the top shelf. None of the dancers came, eaters of meat. The crowd you brought in your train, whom I'll see no more. Sausages this year, all laid out for them. Pumpkins and squashes cooked in the fireplace. I KEPT THANKSGIVING AS YOU LIKED TO SEE IT KEPT. Small comfort that, some comfort that, but small.

And then December comes, December's grey. With thoughts of Christmas, which are thoughts of the children. And of poverty always, it seems, no end to

34

that. What I would buy the children if I could. What I would buy my friends. How I would feed them. The grey turns into green of evergreens. On the Solstice we burn an orange stuck with cloves, in the fireplace, and some kind of color comes back. Mostly the colors of white, and grey, grey-white. The colors of the rivers of New York. The colors of gulls and garbage, and the clothes of the bums. At least winter, when it comes, is all one color. With fire reflected on it. Spring is painful. Is almost as long as Fall, but not quite as long. Summer is blatant colors, blue and green. Is never long enough, neither is winter.

One morning last month woke up glad from some glad dream. To Arione on the phone, saying goodbye. She was leaving for Paris, and then for India. I gave her all my love to weigh her down. Hoping that this way she wouldn't blow away. Told her I'd meet her soon in India, mad itinerary. Coming round from the other side, thru San Francisco. Kyoto, Osaka, Peking, Bankok, Benares. To set out again for Lhasa, or Kathmandu. Some of the holy cities, the names of god. But the navel of the earth for some time was on Ridge Street. Perhaps this bleakness is the shadow of its passing. As the hub o' the universe shifts, & shifts again.

The telephone has become a magic thing. A form of the LSD madness, supercure, the vision. With calls set time back, change the distances, set time ahead, see clearly the arrivals. Three nights ago called George, Alan called George. I was asleep. George has set out. His borrowed time you paid for is over. Would be over, anyway, on the next eclipse. The 18th of December. Clever of him not to wait till the last minute. George has set out at last, they are living at Dean's. He sells his drawings door-to-door in L.A. They will slowly come east, as will Kirby, to do the work. The work will be done, somehow, tho not so well. George said, how he'd meant to tell Freddie the *Blossom* painting was his dancing. The curves, the no straight lines, the grace, the monotony and subtlety of it, are of Freddie's dancing, as it was last spring, spring 1964, when George was here. When he watched you dance a lot.

Thank you, for this Thanksgiving, for the joy here. The people, Huncke, Aila, Erin, Clive, feeling at home, and safe, the children dancing. The rock-and-roll, and 8mm cartoons. The house wrapped us round with love, you were here, wrapped us round with love. Humming a little and getting in the way.

I have set out, I shall buy my press. It shall be here before the winter solstice. There is the store Alan found to put it in. A little cold and white, a bit like Alan. But there is joy in that; the theatre, I think sometimes, is a bit like me. With its red satin curtains, warm Steuben glass. They are both on East Fourth Street, across from each other. I shall play Susan McSween and play in *The Feast*. I shall be at the theatre every day. And at the press, and in my study here. I have set out, beyond the circle you closed. The store for the press is downstairs, half a flight. And back, off the street. Back exit. I shall put in a desk ,and sit at it. Run the machine, build shelves. To the glory of god. And the joy of all sentient beings. As it falls. Outside, around us, almost against the windows. Charred beams, and bricks and glass. The lumpish ruins of this civilization. In which to dig, with a stick, from which to pick the shards.

Thanksgiving on Houston Street one like the other, 1958, 59, 60, a guilty one. The year of guilt, first year that I slept with Roi. Facing the people who knew and the people who didn't. The knowing all the while it was not good dharma. Why you were mad at me. Jimmy Waring bringing pan forte and red wine. Valda making cucumber salad with dill. Nick's buttermilk curry drink.

Jimmy said, how he meant to tell Freddie he wanted to use him again. To make dances for him, as soon as he felt better. That was the week you were kicking we had no chance to tell you, the next week you were shooting again, then you died.

Kirby Doyle at Big Sur (by Diane di Prima)

John Wieners
(by Diane di Prima)

DeeDee Doyle and Freddie Herko
(photo booth self-portrait)

Michael Goldberg, painter (photographer unknown)

LeRoi Jones (by Leroy Lucas)

Michael McClure in San Francisco (by Diane di Prima)

Diane in Washington Square Park (by Alan Marlowe)

winter

It is hands we are discussing now, the long hands of junkies, incredible the fingers, incredible gestures, the energy shooting out thru the restless fingertips, fantastic, the movement so elegant and so vulgar, Kirby Doyle's hands. Judy Garland's hands in *The Bells Are Ringing*. Your hands, Freddie. John Wieners's hands, which were always a little dirty. He haunts this night. Tonight, one after Solstice, winter moon still large, not full anymore. THREE DAYS AFTER FREDDIE'S BARDO. No night without dreams anymore. No sleep tonight. Heater rattles a little overhead, making music. Bed has one sheet, cat paws and boot marks on it. I wait for sleep, its touch, your touch. Two nights ago dreamed of a mandala on fire made of our bodies, our heads were toward the center, bodies (legs) radiating out like a sun wheel. Allen Ginsberg's hair was already catching fire. He was smiling beatifically. WE WERE ALL CLUSTERED THERE, somehow. "Ocean-like congregation." OK.

This is Winter, this rain, this moon, the sounds in the house. Alex banging his head against the top of his crib, sounding like somebody pounding on the door. You are still the fact I live with, this is winter. We tried to make another solstice feast. But could not say the rituals. Burned a birch log to the sun, which came reluctantly back. There are earthquakes everywhere. And winds, storms, disaster areas. I think of Frank, thinking of whoever he thinks of. Leaning, perhaps against a window frame, thinking. I envy him the clarity, the apparent directness. This is Winter. There is snow on the ground, not much, and dirty. I have bought the children new boots with fur inside. I see them, and me, sleeping on subway ramps. Shivering a little. Another winter. I fear it. It comes. I called them my brown mouse and my grey mouse and put them to bed. My girls with big eyes like war movie waifs.

And winter for me is walking on subway grates. So the warm air comes thru and into your shoes. Winter for me is standing in front of heaters, in front of ovens, stoves, and fireplaces. Knowing you should be doing something else. But standing there instead, simply standing there. And keeping warm. As if that was all of life. The end of my existence. To be warm, and a little drowsy. My heater rattles, it takes care of me. Alan is typing on the other side of this wall. He raises funds for his theatre, I have my press. A man is coming tomorrow to look at our house. Perhaps to buy it out from under us. It is cold outside, I think of packing my books. Debbie Lee fell in this first snow and tore her leg muscle. Mini says "Freddie jumped out of a window, and Debbie fell down." Making some link. You are the blank wall I come to every turn. Wherever I start thinking.

But I shall tell of the winters, the thousands of winters. There have been more winters than springs, or summers, or falls. No matter where I start. But tell you first of the falls I didn't mention. The fall I moved to the McClure's pad, '61. A house on Fourth Street, filled with their New York spirits. Reluctant, slow spirits, living in darkness a lot. I turned on all the lights. I moved into the center room and sat there. Sat reading on the bed, with my knees drawn up. Waiting to somehow fill the rest of the space. Listened all night to the voices outside, this was first floor front. To the sounds of the neighborhood, frightened as a cat. Ready to jump any-time in any direction.

That year you came and got me for Thanksgiving. You and Alan, who was still your roommate. Came, moving dishes and pots back to Houston Street. Where I cooked a magic meal for incredible people. The first of the A-heads and Alan's Colombian lovers. Reluctantly cooked that dinner, had planned on a restaurant. But you and Alan came with a shopping cart. Came, swearing that that home was the only kind of Thanksgiving. And so I cooked, Ann Holt made one huge salad. Cutting the lettuce into symmetrical shapes. You all rehearsed *Faust Foutu* in the midst of the party. Crept home to sit the winter out on Fourth Street. Getting all the time bigger with Mini. Belly growing. We had a Christmas there, a Christmas tree. A lot of people drunk, Gregory Corso obnoxious. Cordula von Something waking Roi on the bed. Asking him *why* he was drunk, most petulantly. Fell asleep that New Year's Eve at 10 p.m., which pray god I can still do, it makes my head spin. To think of sleeping that much, dreaming or not.

The other fall I wanted to tell you about was the one before last, 1962. Alan and I joined forces, prepared to flee. We decided to leave on the Last Day of Quest, September 25th. Arrived at the airport of an unknown city. Streets with purple mountains in mist at the ends of them. Innumerable, ungainly, silly palm trees. Wally Berman like some hulking Indian. Wearing silver rings with turquoise, talking little. The pad we stayed in, cushions on the floor. Wind coming thru the boards. Magic little Mini. The drive up the coast to the house that was waiting for us. Walks on the beach, rocks at one end, the cliffs on the other. Learning not to feel trapped by this, there was nowhere to walk to. No more than four miles, one way or the other. Those hills at night, writing in that parlor window. The finding again my century, candlelight. Reading Shelley to Alan, the two of us talking all night.

It was on the beach I said I would marry him. The LaMontes were also living in our house. We drove back down the coast a day or so later. And to New York.

And on the way back again, the slowness of its changing into winter. How I hated Alan on the Jersey Turnpike. Having neglected my dreams, and not seen Roi. Not spoken to him, come and gone like a ghost. The seeing you here, so thin, a little mad. And saying to Jimmy "Make Freddie stop taking amphetamine." Jimmy said no. And I knew then he was right. You were peeling down, stripping to an archetype. The Gypsy King. Whom we found when we returned.

Layer on layer slips by, the seasons change. That year we spent the solstice on the road. Somewhere in Texas. Drove into L.A., into a Winter city. A few days before Christmas. Made a Christmas, some sort of Christmas, out there at the Herms's. Dreamed a lot, slept a lot, pregnant with Alexander.

Last year the solstice was a joyous thing. The wind that filled the house. The songs we made. And prayers. Merce has no demons, or so he told us. The rest of us burned their names in the fireplace. This year to drive out spirits might have meant you, too. We didn't even try to say the prayers. Austerity and sadness, set in like those dreary red sunsets.

Do you recognize your shadow in my face?

This December 25th, this Christmas night, Jeanne sleeps on the floor by the fire, a sad waif, looking a little Egyptian, symmetrical, sad, her two hands under her head. The giant teddy bear beside her that Alan gave her, the Christmas tree lighted, I built her a fire and went upstairs. Knowing it was my sadness she carried there. My missing of your person. And I must learn to think of this some other way. As the great gift, the glorious sacrifice. Made in time by the willing victim, making all things possible for us, and open to us. Sol Invictus, whom we served badly this year. With too much planning. I think about Kirby out there, living on the street in L.A., what kind of Christmas, waiting trial, and know I should call George and do nothing and neither. I clean the typewriter keys, thinking about the books I shall make this year. Cleaning the type. Tomorrow I'll go and look at the store I rented. Put things up on the walls, sweep it a little. See if the gas is hooked up, and the hot water faucet. Small things I shall do them the best I can, and for you. Is that what taking refuge in Kali means?

On Wednesday night I was sick again, with that sickness of stomach. And slept, and dreamed of you, you were Hercules. You had been among the women, that labor was all done, and now your second you were to be a galley slave for Charon. To row that boat across the Styx and back. We came to the pier, to the water's edge, I was with you, and got into the boat. But it turned out the boat drifted into some large calm water, a lake of some sort we were on a Renoir excursion. You said you often came here because it was quiet. You told me you were soon going to take that trip—it seemed to Mexico. A big trip, you said. You asked me to come. We were off the boat again, walking along waterfronts. I said I couldn't, I had to stay, help Alan, spoke of the children, said you know there IS such a thing as dharma. You smiled and said "Where's your sense of adventure, di Prima?" We walked thru the city, stopping here and there, you were leaving in the morning on the trip.

And I wonder if you left, even yet, if you've embarked. For avalon, or for another body. Whatever. Or if you're still hanging about, waiting another right, perfect incarnation. Enjoying your Desire Body to the fullest. Flitting here and there on a wish…

Small things, I think about last Christmas night. And remember nothing of it, though I remember Christmas Eve quite well. Your flitting in with gifts, in those Michael Malce boxes, golden papers. From Florence. I still have them, two of them. One of them has a bundle of papers and pictures. Alan typed a card that says "From the estate of Frederick Herko, February 23, 1937–October 27, 1964." There are jewels with feathers also in that box. Last year you brought it here with a fine jewelled headband. Which was my Christmas present, I've yet to wear it. But love it very much. That band is there, somewhere in my wooden Treasure Chest, next to the box. Your bundles of presents, one for each of us. The gallons of eggnog. Joel knocking over the tree. Nick trying to make the lights work, afraid of electricity, Frankie Francine coming very late. Jack Smith sitting on my bed while I sulked a little, telling me of his loves and fights with Stanley. Stanley and he long split up now.

Nick where? You dead. Joel too drunk to get here anymore. An old lush, getting grey. Bret lazy, then and now, putting an ornament or two on a low-down branch.

Since then have shown up Dirty Mike and Bobi. After all those strange and intervening years. Debbie Lee came last night in a forties dress. Looking rather silly, but a bit less sad.

The Christmas before that, 1962, we spent at the Herms's house, in mysterious woods. In a great silent canyon in Southern California. Among the buzzing insects, it not too cold for them. Louise and I up all night making packages and wrapping things in the dark by candlelight. The tree, with the ornaments we drove from the East. In the back of that old white Ford. Alan stirring slightly, but sleeping for three days. Exhausted by that trip, not so young as he had been. George happy in those days, confident, working a lot. Mini a mite, barely six months old. The indescribable dirt of those sheets, the poor-food we ate. How angry Alan was not to be in our new house. With no gas, no lights, no heat, no running water. Feeling if I truly loved him I'd move in. Right then, before Christmas, and no nonsense about it. Our trip to town on Christmas Eve for presents. The five and dime in Santa Monica. Frightening, frightening, I saw James Mason in Westwood. A tired old man with crazy eyes. The gentle magic of that Christmas morning. How Jeanne had blossomed under all that love. That was the best Herms time, we were all so happy. Alex a dim and constant nausea.

And the Christmas before in that East Fourth Street pad. Where Alan and you came, days before, to deck the

51

tree. And Alan left angry hating Christmas always. And Christmas Eve, when Alan gave you boots. All kinds of clothes things and you wept for joy. Knowing you were loved and cared for, all you wanted. All I want now, if it comes not, I die. As you did. To feel wrapped warm in someone else's cloak. A simple thing.

That year on Fourth Street Gregory Corso drunk and pugnacious, with a retinue of girls. Cordula von Some-body waking Roi up on my bed. "But why WHY" she wanted to know "don't you feel good? Have you been DRINKING?" How he put her on. How mad she was at me, at pregnant me. Looking me in the eye, asking why wasn't Hettie there. How you and Alan wrapped me warm that night. On that old black couch in the cor-ner of the front room. Nick and Billy full of Romular on the floor. Watching Roi tease the life out of Cordula, Mini stirring a little inside me. Did Ann Holt come that night? I think she did. And sat on my double bed in a gorgeous huge fur coat.

And the years before, on Houston Street, run together. I remember only one as a separate thing: 1959, with Zella there, and Roi. Roi trying to find out how things stood with me. Bringing for present a Chinese firecracker. Which exploded with colored streamers we hung on the tree. Just before he knocked on my door and we made first love.

The year Jeanne was an infant I don't remember. 1957. Were Mo and Pauli there? I think they were. I think you were with Ed Royce, but I don't know.

I remember though Christmas 1958. That was with Bret and Bernice and Mitch. Bret going into the army a few days later. Candles and dinner in my little living room. Which doubled as a bedroom. Jeanne could walk and talk by then. That oil painting of a harlequin made by one Don of Don & Kitty. Long since vanished. People and painting both. Mitch taking pictures, all of us making talk.

One year, but which? made a whole lot of Christmas Eve fishes. Red snapper, and especially eel, the sacred Christmas fish. To the consternation of Jimmy Waring. The fishes quickly eaten, off that old drawing table. The wine, a festival as it should be.

Well I remember the tree of Amsterdam Avenue. The chains of paperclips, the hanging fountain pens, old necklaces. Whatever would make glitter. We never had lights. There was the fire, my fountain pen twisted a little on its cord. O'Meara skillful at this, and wrapping presents.

And back to the year we got Bobi Schwartz a room. 1954. In that old hotel no one of us knows the name of. It used to be over Whelan's, was called The Ashtray. And bought him tacky dishes from the Mexican shop. And tacked his pictures up on the wall, got a small tree. Moved in his books, and papers. We had no place to live soon after that. Bobi took us into another place he'd gotten. Somewhere on West Tenth Street, in the Lenny's Hideaway district. In those days I didn't know you, or not well. You still lived in Ossining, studied music, were fat.

Christmas 1953, my first Christmas away from home, in that silly apartment on Fifth Street, I don't remember at all. I made it for Lori.

Christmas 1952 I sat in a bar, in Arthur's Tavern, on Sheridan Square, with O'Meara and Lori and promised them I'd leave school, leave home and take an apartment with them. We were scared. A few days after that I broke the news, my folks had literal fits, swallowed tongues, threw me around the room, and I moved out. Slept that New Year's Eve in a hallway with Joan O'Meara. After a party at Gaby's in Mount Vernon. She was very sorry, but there was nowhere we could stay. Learned a lot the difference between heated and unheated hallways. Hall-ways with couches. Hallways at least with rugs. Hall-ways with lots of bells so you could ring one. Get in, and duck behind the stairs for a while. And then get com-fortable. Hated very much sleeping on marble steps. On account they were cold. And always drafty. Discovered, however, how to sleep on steps, curled up the body falls naturally onto three levels. One of the advantages of being short.

Beyond that they all extend, the Christmases at home. With only silver ornaments, only blue lights. Mysterious trees, ceiling-high, blue-lighted in the dark. Wreaths on the doors. Areaways full of snow. Decca 78 albums, "Christmas in Song." Got them last year from Brooklyn, tried to play them. But only broke the needle on the phonograph. Too many cracks and scratches. Have them still. The green rug, faded, the blue light, the strufoli. Jovial uncles. Liqueurs. Ladies a little tipsy, not used to drinking. The endless mysterious joy of that Brooklyn house. When it was four floors high, with a spiral staircase. The first step of the second flight creaked a lot. The ghosts that stood by my bookcase, the skeleton on fire that followed me up the stairs (that was earlier), the fireplace (mantel) that asked "Diane, Diane, Diane, will you die?" when I went by. Mysterious marble ladies naked with fruits, holding up the mantels decking the hot air system. Long since gone too. Those long, unfurling Christmases. Lasagna. Clothes that I hated. Books that I always read. The ugly upright piano out of tune. The one blue book of Christmas carols, we had traced over the letters on the cover so many times that they had all come out. "Away in a Manger" first carol in the book. Plunking them out, and all the family singing.

Christmas after Christmas. Merry Christmas, Freddie, be good. (Jeanne thinks this too.) So is sage in the Bardo. Leave it as soon as you can. Don't drag this out, though I'll miss you. Merry Christmas. The season of feasts is almost over for us.

It is New Year's Eve, and I have been typing on a book of poems to you. That and another book Alan edited of my early poems. A job I gave him this summer, he was so listless, so sulky and bugged, George gone, me in my book, so I said "edit a book of my early poems," and I have been typing them up. But the names and faces run thru my head, what is it about New Year's Eve? For me it is not even the true new year, that comes for me on the Solstice, and yet New Year's Eve is New Year's Eve no matter what. It must be the energy in the air, the expectation, the excitement and sadness all

55

around us, here on this avenue so quiet you'd think we wouldn't even be aware of it, and yet we are, we right here are most susceptible to those things, this is a way-side inn. And so I stopped, and found the old paper I use specially for this book (Kirby and I know how that is, what fetishists writers are, one paper for each kind of writing, and which pen when, and which ink). The faces float by so fast.

Kirby, for instance, whose trial was today and we have not heard from him and what does that mean, does that mean that he's in jail? I think not, yet don't know, and so think if I don't hear by Monday I'll call his lawyer out there and find out… And Jim Elliott, for no reason at all, saw a photo he did of birds over the sea, it's on my wall, and I think of his warm clean welcome couches, the setting out from Topanga I did in his place, the Easter party he came to at our house out there… And then Audre, I think of calling her, but the lines are so busy, hard to get thru, and then, isn't that what everyone does, call people on New Year's Eve, and it's better some-how to sit here typing. John Wieners, and, of course, last New Year's Eve. Where were you then? Not here. The LSD, my first. Jimmy and John McDowell arguing about little boys. The round table emerging as a possession of ours thru so many lives. As the blue flames emerged. As I was born. Knowing this was the most important thing that had ever happened to me. Trying to force a sugar cube down Jimmy's throat. John Wieners here then, and Mo, too. How each year is different. The cycle too long to be repeated within our memory. Tonight went to Sing Wu's with Alan. Then tried to get into the St. Marks to see a movie. *The Sun Also Rises*, but they wouldn't let us in. Too late, they said, the box office is closed. Not but go in anyway. Not taking the money and pocketing it, just no. Alan sits in his grey chair making money lists. His statue of Krishna dances, in the light of a candle. The shadow on the wall behind. My Shiva is encased in flames. The reflection thru the red glass on the metal. Which surrounds him.

This year I will buy a flute and a piece of jade. Will perform in every program at that theatre. Will print at least a book a month. Maybe more. Write occasional verse and this long whatever to you. Keep a journal too. Buy one day after tomorrow.

We are hearing Mahler. I bought Mahler for Alan for Christmas. But he doesn't like it as much as I do. It's the fifth symphony, and not so pyrotechnic as the second. Like flames. Alex is asleep downstairs. Your mandala is over his crib. Alan says you gave it to him in the funeral parlor. One way or another you did. He is your child too. As are always Jeanne and Mini. Jeanne who talks to you in her candlelight. As do I, and dream of you at night. I DO NOT WANT TO KEEP YOU IN THE BARDO. Get out, as soon as you can. My womb is quiescent. You probably will have to find another.

Jeanne who talks to you, as I do too. As did my grandmother, for eleven years. To a picture of my grandfather in her bedroom. Night after night, before she could go to sleep. They thought her a little demented, my father and mother. But I see where she was, what more natural than tell you what's going on.

I remember New Year's Eve in Topanga Canyon. After that strange Christmas with the Herms's. Our house so cold, and bare, and dismal. Formal. The most depressing house I ever lived in. The grimmest countryside in the world. And that night, the children sleeping, Alan and I looking at TV a little. Going to bed at ten, in the empty hills. The feeble sounds at midnight, people clomping around, over and thru the bushes. The noisemakers, bottles breaking, all so far away. And yet, on the same hill, right outside our house. Alan thinking of Indians creeping to the door. Our sleep together on that narrow couch.

Or the New Year's Eves at LeRoi Jones's houses. The one for which I bought a black velvet dress (1960?). The one on which I was pregnant with Mini. Meeting Nicky Thacher there. Big Ray Johnson, one of those years, in the snow with me. Holding 3 a.m. an umbrella over my head. Helping me get a cab. Saying nothing, a large, black, stolid, good presence, who knew my grief.

The New Year's Eve I made at Jimmy Waring's. We all making collages from the collage box. In his tiny apartment on 20-something Street. Pasting our way thru midnight and into the new.

The one I spent in Lenny's Hideaway with Bobi Schwartz. O'Meara and I, watching all those men kissing at midnight. Looking so strange and pathetic in suits and ties. Confetti in the air, fell on the bar. Streamers, and weeping. The jukebox played on and on.

The one I ventured out with Bret to Downey's. Was Ben with us too? We picked up a stray actor and gave him a New Year's. A thing to do, somehow. Took him home with us to Amsterdam Avenue. The steak in Downey's more than I'd eaten in months.

When I was a child they always woke me at midnight. The heavy sadness of those 40s years. The war. The drinking, noisemakers. Pajamas with feet. My mother kissing me desperately and weeping. The radio, the house full of people speaking Italian. The year they let me sleep thru and I couldn't forgive them.

Now I have, for the first time, allowed myself the task of your suffering. The contemplation of that, amid the scatter and chaos of my life. How much it restores to us. How you prayed to Arione, the night before. Hoping some blacker secret might save you yet. You and Jeanne running together down windscattered streets. I have looked on the fact that you might have been in pain. Those black preceding weeks. Admitted this. You prayed to Arione on the roof of Kirby Doyle's house. You conjured Kirby under those murky stars. I passed John Allessandro on another street. When I should have been at your party. I wonder now if you cared that no one came. I allow myself to hurt, to see you hurt. To see you bewildered, tormented, your smile / in the coffin / comes back now and wipes this out.

The other night we smoked DMT on parsley. Out of Lenny's pipe, we sat by our living room fire, amid the debris and horror of burned-out Christmas. Taking down the tree, but not on Epiphany. Not as we should have, burning it, but simply taking down the tree. It seemed to me I would never exorcise you, in this house, out of this house. YOU SPREAD OUT IN THE AIR HERE. I tried to see next Christmas, a blur, not here, not anywhere else. I came upstairs, found that Alan's desk was burning. The Altar to the Void had split in two.

My life has split in two. Cleft. By the leap. I hold the present and future in one hand, the past in the other, patiently, endlessly trying to mesh the edges. To make some sense of it. To bridge. TO BRIDGE. No go. They slip in and out of different dimensions. The one becomes invisible when I turn to look at the other. Yet thinking of seashells in the rocks of the western mountains, the sea pebbles embedded in the soil some 8,000 feet in the air, I am comforted somewhat. As if the bridge will grow, will spin itself. Out of this intermittent buzzing pain.

Snow today, cold feet, wet boots and tiredness. Wind. How many winters we had endured together. How many winter soups we had devoured. Mini struggles into taxis to nursery school. Slipping on ice, hating wind going up her nose. As Jeanne did before her. The rituals of sleeping thru a snowfall. Warm bed, the silence of the stopped city. The world one color. As in primeval chaos. Chaos is quiet.

I spend long hours on theatre mailing lists. Which you warned me against in our last dream together. I gather up my poems to you. I pray. The press is in the shop, the shop is yellow. Tomorrow I learn to run it, after that. Book after Book. To change the face of time.

I am weary, I could weep when I think of us. How much more there is to do, we won't make it this time. Have to come back again, all of us, finish it off. One

time, or twice, or three. Depending on so many turnings. Jimmy. Alan. Gratuitous states of grace. I think of
the Golden Monastery in Nepal. The only place I truly
want to be born. How much to finish between this and
that. How clear your leap was the statement "Not this
time." Now Kirby takes that stance. Ignoring the life he
glimpsed here on the east side the navel of the earth he
seeks death. Another body to try and make it in. Filling
the pores and all the holes of this one with methedrine,
endless unsavory elixir.

George too, they have given up trying to make it out.
What is called middle age, perhaps. Buses, stars, wind
are the sounds here. I feel us spinning off. I cling to my
press, it weighs 900 pounds. And hope that is enough to
weigh me down.

This is the gift, that my life has split in two. Stop trying
to mesh it, really let it go. The part that comes off, let it
float away. DETACHMENT, like everything else, a word to
be taken literally. As Alan will leave me, and later the
children will go. As I will lose everything and gain, perhaps, myself. To stand in the clear spring light and say
I am Shiva. Intoning. The pigeons will look down on
me. My brick wall outside, my nest will grow more in-
ward. This is your gift too, you constantly cut me loose.
Gnawing at all the ropes that hold me down. "Where's
your sense of adventure, di Prima?"

I hear you in the snow outside the door. You scratch at
the door, you want some lentil soup. You rattle the mail-
box flap, the wind comes in. Wisps of you float up the
stairs and spread in the air. You spread like a blanket,

filling the air with warmth. I grow safe and sleepy, I shall go to sleep soon, thank you.

Roi has returned to my side, we run machines together. We do not touch, we spin a cocoon of warmth. And live inside of it. This too is a gift from you, begun in Topanga. Begun the winter morning you looked out of your window on Houston Street, and into my kitchen window and saw my hand hold out a coffee cup, and saw a dark hand take the cup from me, and knew that Roi had stayed the night with me, karma was all fucked up, you were angry at me. Angry for days (two or three) while I wrassled with it. Wrote poems, wrote The Jungle, The Ballroom and The Party. Dwelt in that love as in the hand of God.

And you gave absolution, began to teach us whatever we could learn of a life together. A gift of yours, to us. Still not completed. The means have come to hand to make some light. Goodnight little brother, dear love, in the dull grey snow. Come, kiss us all goodnight,
I'll spin
        some kind of rest.

Last night I went with Alan to look at our new theatre. Red walls, red satin curtains, a theatre made by someone who loves theatres. Who loves old theatres. The wrought iron work on the seats something you should see, you would delight in it. The silence and space of even a small theatre at night. The spaces. You filled them somehow. Your strident, demanding voice, your habit of moving incessantly, talking incessantly. The way you would have tried out the stage, all your advices, mostly unsought and unheeded. What a Dancer Needs, spelled out, again and again. That bag of rags that we threw scornfully out. Not even looking into it for schmattas. The hundreds and hundreds of theatres we worked in together. Off Bowery Gallery, always cold, Joanna having hysterics on that black stage. About the cold, and her hepatitis. The fights you and Alan had in the back of that house. Black walls, no heat ever in the radiators. John Wieners arriving shy to see his play. You and I playing *Discontent of the Russian Prince* together. The waits alone together while the lights dimmed. Before we went on in the dark and got into bed. You used to throw away your most gorgeous speech "How beautiful I am..." Typing it recently, I realized how much more beautifully you'd have done it last year. Playing it unembarrassed, all of it. Remember that thing called Ballet '57? The masks we fashioned in Eddie Johnson's loft. Night after the afternoon I got pregnant with Jeanne. A chilly February down on Prince Street. A silly ballet, and pompous, but the leap, that Jeannie Thomas made, was something else. The Master Institute, the Living Theatre with its creaking light board, New Bowery last year where you always came late. How you came late when you danced for Sergio. A great breathtaking dance, a dance of power. Your chant at the end of it, your face, not made up, but painted. A mask again, but this time gold, coral, turquoise, something else.

It is in the theatre that I will miss you. In all the great, empty theatres, dead of night, where we will be, Alan and I, again and again. Perhaps for the rest of this trip. All echoing.

The night you came to the Bleecker Street Theatre to work. To fashion, in George's set, an evening of dancing. How you kept misplacing the props and I threw you out. Because *The Blossom* was to open in two days and I needed order there (stage manager-ish). All the actors were hysterical, I needed order. You played the piano a long time, and then you left. You never danced there later.

The air of our new theatre is filled with the things you would have made. Is this an indulgence?

January 20, 1965. It is a spring day, one of those spring days they give us in the middle of Winter, between one snowstorm and the next. The kind of day we would perhaps have ventured out, years ago, for Breakfast Out, an event, imagining the trees already beginning to bud in Central Park, our shoes getting full of muddy water. It will freeze up again, and snow again. I am reading tonight at the Stryke Gallery. I wish I could invite you to the reading. But feel you gone, into some other womb, capped tight, waiting the bright awareness you will bring with you this time, still at its center. Alan paces and makes money calls, we are building a stage that curls around the audience. I come from so far each day, to try to help him. Albert Fine works away at the other typewriter, in Alan's cold gold room, under the eaves. Writing long skinny poems to Ray Johnson. I am moving away and out from a spinning center. To be cast off, finally, like a drop of water. Last night spoke for hours to Vancouver mystic, in Paradox restaurant, who read my palm. Came back to a beautiful Alan at table, like a Mongolian demon in

Nepalese show last summer. Hair streaming upwards, face downwards, he having just landed from sky travel on mountaintop. Astonished, ingenuous demon, turquoises in hair. Me old landtraveler, fond of yaks, learning painstakingly to walk on water. Maybe later to fly peak to peak. Short distance, anyway, not rivalling dakinis. How many Winters this kind of day brought rejoicing. I stop now, to light candle to my small god, to light incense, to perhaps set the room(shrine) in order. Waiting all the time for the hot water to heat up. To take ritual spring bath, with bubbles, for the weather...

At the study window huge icicles make me crystal draperies. Blunt now at points, thick, like German sculpture. Not the airy French-form tapestries they were the day the snow came. So many things are easy to renounce. I stand astonished. Made increasingly aware of how many things there *are* to renounce. One day, one day. Boy in Paradox read my palm said age 45 you give all up take long trip. No said give all up 45, long trip at 50. Sounded about right, all the children grown. Alan well launched, spreading his magic, lights and tinsel. The sport/game/play. The Dance. How late you were last year, at the New Bowery Theatre. The night you danced for Sergio, and yourself. And Billy Morrow and Eric Brunn, whoever. All suicides. The night you danced for Sergio, wearing a painting on your face, illuminated before a mirror, held in your hand. Kirby called last night. He is clean. Clean of that little girl, and clean of smack. He calls, time after time, to ask for you. But doesn't do it quite. George has yielded to flesh, lives in the woods. There are so many lives. They stretch mercifully before us. To rectify.

Alan rushes up, demanding phone numbers. Impatient, heavy with projects, plans, I stop, go downstairs, which he has filled with smoke. By putting big wood on the fire with no little. Not enough paper, either, to make it catch. I tell him a phone number, go away again, wondering how you did it, this theatre thing. Wondering how I do it. Not too well. Not, probably, well enough. Wanting as I do only candles, incense, quiet. To study, to write to you, to meditate. To have a bell, and small but sacred mirror. Fires, and silence around me. The trip in. The sun has resigned, has given enough of spring. At least for the moment. My icicles turn white, lose their gold and transparency. I can do nothing in that impatient world that pushes and tugs at me, from all directions. I keep on waiting for it to go to the theatre.

I should be remembering winters, should I not? This was to be a book of remembrances. But this winter catches me up, all winters are the same winter, all springs are different from each other, and summers too. And falls, in their deaths are different. But winters the same. It snows. It does not snow. One stays at home. As much as one is able, stays at home. The house is always cold, whichever house. Either because the landlord gives no steam. Or because there is no central heating. Those are the best. They are always cold but always warm in some places. Here it is the heater in the kitchen. And the study, which is warm no matter what. Not as warm as I would like, but warm enough. The search always for the way to get the feet warm. And the hands. And the tip of the nose. I think I must have been a dog, the tip of my nose is always cold. I think I have been warming it up for thousands and thousands of years. I used to at night put it in the back of whoever was sleeping beside me. They would jump. I would feel with my cheek the cold place I had made on their warm backs. But now I sleep alone, much of the time. In my study, my head to the east, facing the little god on the wooden altar. And the nose, the feet, and the ends of the hands are cold. At Amsterdam Avenue the warm place was fireplace. You sat there, day after day, with Joan O'Meara. Wrapped in that motley afghan I had made. Your first attempt at schmatta, gypsy king. Not knowing it yet. O'M burned the toes of her sneakers, warming her feet. You both would huddle, waiting for some hot soup.

The kitchen was warm there too, but very greasy. And full of garbage and roaches. One didn't go there much except to eat.

But the fireplace was the place, that first year there we pulled the big bed out, in front of the fire. And slept in it, five of us, huddled, all lying on one side. Fitting like spoons. If one of us wanted to turn, the whole row stirred, woke a little, and turned on their other side. The wonderful nights when one of us was waking. We took turns, all night long, to keep the fire. Those nights when it was five degrees or less. The silence, while all of you slept, and the wood dropped slowly. Turning to coals in the grate, and I put more on top. Read Virgil, or Ovid, added more wood on top. Heard your breathing, heard the wind, the trucks outside. Feeling their way on the ice. Aware of the wind, the river, the smokestacks. All only yards from the door. Mysterious comings and goings at the shoe factory. The wide, quiet streets, the candlelight on my book. How we took turns being the others' guardian angels. Each filling the room with love and firelight. Drawing, or writing letters, or turning pages. The cats awake beside one.

The steam on the windows at Houston Street. The shadows. That flitted by outside, four stories up. The chill in the large front room on East Fourth Street, where the heat was never enough, and there was wind. The winter that I spent there I spent in bed. Reading under the covers, switching the book hand to hand, one hand staying warm.

Breathe. Breathe deep in the cold. This much I've learned. And pass it on to you, for your next trip. Don't huddle, breathe down to your cock, breathe in the winter. As it turns to life in you, it turns to love. Incandescent air! Bright spirit, always sustaining us! WHEN WE MOVE THRU THE AIR, WE MOVE THRU THE BODY OF KALI. CAST ASIDE ALL CLINGING, AND THE ESSENCE WILL EMERGE. THE BEST TIME FOR MONEY IS 10:30 TO 12:30. Says Alan loudly, from the other room. Albert answers politely. I must pick up Mini, at school.

I remember a winter snow when we set out, laughing, in our thin shoes for a walk, several of us, Bret and Dirty Mike among others. Spun down the endless empty blocks in the wind. Falling time after time in the wet, rolling in snow. The wind. As we should have done when children. We were children. A downstairs luncheonette celled Francine's. Near all those dreary, lovely rehearsal studios that filled 56th Street. (And the winter we sat in Rienzi's, O'Meara and I, sipping hot chocolate and watching the snow outside. When a large, sad mulatto boy we knew, one Big Bruce, not to be confused with Young Bruce, came wandering in, and pulled his hand out of his dirty trench coat pocket. Which hand was covered with blood from a slit wrist. Said Bruce, sadly, "My pockets are full of blood." We got him outside before they threw him out, copping Rienzi napkins on the way. Made high school tourniquets with napkin and pencil. Tried to stanch the bleeding, standing there in the snow, all our toes numb. Then wrapped the wrists with the napkins. sent him on his way. Only to find him seeking us, hours later, in the Minetta Tavern up the block. Gave in, took him home to Fifth Street, he went to bed. Delirious, babbling of rats on water pipes. In the cellar where he'd been living, having no pad and no job. First forced some soup down his throat in some village restaurant. Then put him to bed, filled him with sleeping pills and went to the movies. Came home, he had waked up, gave him more pills. He was babbling on about his mother and sister. Sixteen-year-old runaway who lived with us said she'd sleep on the floor tonight, thank you, she didn't want to wake up in the morning next to a corpse. Cheerful thought, we thought, and climbed into bed with Bruce. Said Linda from the floor, as we drifted off, "I think I'm taking it very well for my first suicide."

Morning found Bruce up before us, he'd sawed at his wrists again. Hid all cutting edges, gave him more sleeping pills. On the theory he'd eventually come to his senses. He eventually did. Folksinger friend came to see him, sight of a male friend straightened him up, he got up and went to St. Vincent's. Where they clamped his much abused veins and sent him home. He returned

69

to us, we fed him cold sweet and sour pork in restaurant container. Fitted him out with telephone slugs, he called home. His family, who lived in Worcester, Massachusetts. Gave him all our old pawn tickets to sell, which he did, and took off. A bus to Massachusetts, he's still around. Alive and somewhat kicking.

We breathed a sigh of relief, and turned to our house. A mess it was, us scheduled for eviction. Having just given six hundred dollars to Lori, and not a cent for rent, we packed our things. Spread on the floor old grey sheets, threw things in their centers. I decided I would never again wear a skirt. So left all skirts behind, all clocks, some books. Records. Irons. Toasters. Much, much paraphernalia. Schlepped what was left thru the snow to Bobi Schwartz's. Remember on one trip across the city, stopping on the steps of Cooper Union, the halfway point, with an orange crate full of books and odds and ends. O'Meara and I stopped dead, sat on the steps. Righted the crate, set a candle. holder on top. Behold, it was our room, it was our house. Right there on that windy corner, or wherever, we knew it then, and I still know it now, wherever we sit down and take out the things. Small fetish objects that form altar and hearth.

The walls of our ex-house we filled with delirious inscriptions. Many people came over just to write on them. Over the beige that we had put over the grey that the landlord had left to us when we moved in. Large flowery words and songs and pictures all in indelible pastels before we left. Left an ugly '30s gate-leg table, relic of my mother. Walked back, not too long after, saw the guts of my murdered piano lying in the snow.

January 31. It is Sunday morning, and I have had a bubble bath. In the cold bathroom, filling it with steam from the tub. The outside cold, preparing to snow again, bleak. Bleak. How dirty our necks, our hands, and hair used to get in the winter. Refusing to bathe in those drafty and cold apartments, we became the color of soot from poking the fire. And smelled of bacon or ham—a smoked-meat smell. Clung to our hair and our shoes. No poker, we used the broom handles a lot, which got shorter and shorter, till we burned the broom. But now, more Spartan, or Hindu, I bathe in the frosty rooms. Took clean clothes to the hot heater, to put them on. An old yellow polo shirt of yours, a dancing shirt, terry cloth of some kind, short sleeves, I pulled it on, stopping to pull out a label from village shop which was hanging by a thread. Label read "Leading Man," a brand name which echoed pathetically.

Much colder this year than last, the blankets over the broken window in the kitchen scarcely serve. We leave the oven on as well as the heater, all of the time. I send the children away on the weekends, when I can, so they will warm up, and get cleaned. Think occasionally of you coming in to take showers, eat, the trips to Ratner's or Coscia's, when I had some money. The Sunday mornings last winter I would drop in on you and Debbie. Bringing sometimes some cake, getting some amphetamine. You would have coffee brewing, and bread, sometimes butter, sometimes milk and/or sugar for the coffee, but not often. Quite frequently dry bread, black coffee, it was a feast after the cold trip. A feast too, to get away from the talk of theatre, which last year was so much more frantic, so much just Alan and me. Your itinerary in that apartment. First and for a long time the front room was yours, mirrors and beds, confusion, clothes strewn about, photographs of Nijinsky. Debbie hung David's sad yellow painting in the kitchen. Then finally the little room in back was yours, sometimes alone, sometimes with Arione, that was later, summer at least, or late spring. The little room that you left to go to death. The chaos of it, two days after your jump, when Debbie and I went back to Eleventh Street, to clean it up. Broken jewels, suitcases of pornography, broken staves, flutes that will play for no one else. Pieces of cloth, pieces of tin, your works. Altar cloth gone, gold net hanging in torn strips every-where. My return home, to find Roi here, to be able to tell him "I feel like I'm up to here in blood" indicating my right arm, well above the elbow. Your gift to us of each other, to be able to tell him "I love you still, al-ways love you, it has no logic. You too have your work and world. And there is, repeat is, there is such a thing as dharma." The melting of anger in the heat of your death. Melted anger lubricating the gears of the cos-mos. So many old squeaks gone now.

My press goes round. It is very beautiful, it is printing 15,000 purple theatre flowers. Same flower that we've had from the beginning. That Marian Zazeela made for us. When she was Marian Schleifer, and loved LeRoi. I see us all dead, and beautiful in death. I see someone else taking over at this typewriter. To write these words to us all as the cosmos turns. Well greased with the grease of love, and melted angers.

As Lucinda danced last night. Graceless precision, a certain nakedness. Not fashionable when you did it. As Jimmy acted my monologue to him. His stylization and your nakedness. I remember now in the kitchen at Ridge Street promising to write you a monologue. It was night, there were candles, we talked by the kitchen sink. While Alan and Kirby next room spoke of *The Blossom*. I called up for you my LSD power, it tingled in me, I realized I had no business calling it up, unless to do something with it and so did something. Pressed the tingling palm of my hand against your forehead. Felt you absorb that fire and draw it off. It was then I promised you your monologue. I remember then thinking it would be the monologue of a saint. I shall write it, it shall go like this:

Blasted fore and aft by cocks I stand astride in
the windy park. Little birds peck at my bare
toes, my staff broken off an 1890s bedstead, in
my hand. Wind pulls at it, at my rags, my too
tight lace black panties under my jeans.

The sky takes care of me. I take my refuge in
the hurricane. Which makes lace of my most
undistinguished schematas. I burn with the
cocks that have pierced me, have poured their
life into me. The assholes I have pierced form
an aura about me. I am holy. I walk to Delancey
Street for enchiladas. The Puerto Rican behind the counter recognizes me. He serves me
quickly, salaams and makes obeisance. His dog
lays back his ears against his head and growls. I
lay my staff in my lap and eat a lot.

City of the sun, I walk in the night with my
woman. She white, I black, in rags beneath
the moon. Seeking always abandoned houses,
parking lots. Pausing often to look in garbage
barrels on corners. Singing in the blue light
our minds have made of the air. Dancing from
street to street, our arms full of rhinestones.

My rage stripped off by wind, my fat, my other
face. Left behind, discarded, on an abandoned
roof. Like the ballet I wanted to make in a
swimming pool. Like my beds and paintings,
my clothes, altars, wisdom, jewels. The little
girls I taught. The summer sun. Never to come
again to this stripped-down forehead.

I smile a lot, I am truly hollow within. Wind
buoys me up, sun draws me to itself. Water ca-
resses me. Earth enters all my pores. I say "Take
care of the churches, the witches, the scattered
bricks. Bejewelled zippers, the fires, the hearths.
The children are dead." Or will be, soon, there
is dancing, fix your teeth. Choose the best jewel
for your turban. Turn backward. Make music,
walking backward. WALK INTO THE EAST RIVER
TO BATHE, CRYING OUT TO KRISHNA.

The horizon is opaque, made of pastels. The
hills and cliffs of Jersey, tiffany glass. Cast iron
bums eternally speak of lilies. Tear me loose
from this love, like chunks of inedible chocolate. This new receding substance of our lives.

74

It is February again, and we have a theatre. The weather spins us around, sometimes the golden city of the sun, sometimes that blood-red fog, that evil mist. Been with us on and off since October. It is funny, we are at the same point we were at last February. Last February at the New Bowery Theatre. Not the Off Bowery Gallery, this was a large place, large lobby, very green. Very ugly green, too high, too long and narrow. And filled with ugly fake-Tiffany lamp shades. One beautiful one among them. Crazy landlady, Teddy Bergery always lurking. Like some large Henry James witch, clutching her ragged furs. Annoying us all. Art show full of uglies Michael Malce hung on those green walls. The theatre itself, how we loved it, it was home. Narrow and dark as it was.

Walking there one morning in an icy rain. Under the strain and duress of no money, show troubles. The Bergery lurking and screaming all the time. Walking there thru the desolate streets, deserted, grey. Wind howling. A lady bum with a large, red forehead. Half bald. Large bloated face. Sat on the steps of a deserted building. Swaying and drinking, talking to herself. A truly repulsive creature, hard, cruel face. As well as coarse. Bloated and mean at once. Walked past her sitting in dirty ragged coat, on up to theatre, delivered whatever there, and started back again to the house, rain heavier now. Same lady bum, still there, now joined ludicrously by man bum, who was feeling under her slimy and ragged skirt. While she leaned back in the doorway voluptuously, bottle still in hand. At first repulsion like nausea, so much worse than watching roaches fucking. Then before I reached them, or passed them, a startling and fierce light breaking: IT WAS THE GOD HIMSELF AND

HIS CONSORT THERE IN THE RAIN. Not "as if," not symbol, the God himself, the spot was sacred. That which I witnessed holy, a great blessing. With which I was favored, though I was unworthy. I was shaken, my feet led me on to the house, not my knees. They were weak, I was shaken, for days did not speak of this. For many weeks. The ugly sniveling bum. Some kind of white-ish smear on his blue rag coat. His noises of excitation. The bloated woman. The god and goddess creating the universe. A manifestation, and blessed.

That was the theatre. So hard, such a struggle to stay with it. Being finally locked out, that horror, war with screwdrivers. Or the night the lobby was full of those blue policemen.

And the small safe theatre after, on Bleecker Street. But that was in the spring, with the Hermses here.

That winter, the running to and from that place. The children bedded down, me taking tickets. Or talking to people in the lobby. Greeting, as hostess. While Dorothy Podber stole collages off the walls. While you came late every night. The day that Teddy Bergery came to the house. The horror of seeing her here, on our decrepit staircase. We saw her again this summer, as on the Styx. On the boat to Fire Island, a lonely fury.

Sleet falls. Light falls and sleet. Remy reminiscing on Second Avenue remembered a dance of Jimmy's called *In the Mist*. In which Aileen Passlof carried a lightbulb around. There was a chair. She wore an empire costume. You and Vincent flickered around her, in the light.

Merce dances, growing older, at Hunter College. Viola's foot is gone, is pretty much gone. She'll probably act, make dances instead of dance. Though she doesn't say so yet. Carolyn Brown has added a little fire. Her calm now reminiscent of Plizetskaya. Remy envious and dour sat behind us.

The February before this, '63, Clive Matson blew in from New York to visit us, skinny and young. Hitchhiked across the country in the snow. On the way to visit his family, near L.A. He hid in Alan's Ford, wrote poems in there, while Alan and I fought in the kitchen, throwing old cups at the walls. Then we all took off for the north. Driving all night arrived in San Francisco. Where it rained, ceaselessly. Howling winds. We slept at the McClure's on the floor. The apple trees near Daly City were blooming. Later letters from New York showed Clive's picture of Alan and me. How happily married we were, thrashing everything out.

That was my first escape from Topanga Canyon, my poverty-ridden, grisly life with Alan. The second, not much later, you were there, and we drove up the coast of California together. You arrived, brown and happy at our door, from Mexico, with Michael Malce who looked like an American Indian. We rented a station wagon. Put the children on a mattress in the back. Michael held Mini a lot. The sea beneath us. You driving, getting us lost among eucalyptus. In the wind. The beach we stopped at to dance, while you played your flute. All of us quite turned on, a young boy we had picked up enchanted, his first pot, the wind, waves breaking. The lighthouse, rocks out a ways white with seal droppings and bird droppings, the air filled with the cries of the creatures, you and Jeanne scrambling down the rocks to some caves full of abalone shells, coming back with your hands full of treasures. And the beach where the sand was black, us stopping the car and leaning over to watch the white line of foam on the blackness. Jade Cove. Lucia. Magic all around us.

We stayed in a magic house on Laguna and Post. Street names in San Francisco resonating. In Marilyn Rose's house, she lived in one tower. The children and I slept on endless mattresses. I filled the house with groceries, bought with Michael's money. We visited Michael McClure. Malce sat outside in the station wagon. In the San Francisco rain, having shyness and one of his fits. McClure came downstairs to greet him, to coax him out. I took Marilyn out of the house to the thrift shops. Seeking a present for Alan who we left behind. Saw a Bob Branaman show with a magic pink and gold drawing. When we set out for Topanga again, car battery had to be replaced. Michael Malce was angry and sulked.

Topanga was full of fog and birds, and the fir tree outside our front window made Japanese pictures. Topanga was full of pot, and quarrels, and boredom. You went back east. Left us with Billy Linich. We returned soon after, in the spring.

The February before that, plays again. Or plans for plays, a series we never did. Alan took off for Boston with the money, you came to live on Fourth Street and wept all night. We opened in March, in the spring, at the Maidman Theatre.

And the February before that (climbing downstairs backwards, like the Ida Lupino movie we ran backwards at John McDowell's house last Fall) Roi and I made our first *Floating Bear*, lived in a tentative, hung-up world of gesture. February is always a hard month to get thru. Harder than January, though January seems much harder. That's the trick of it. One is unprepared for the hardness of February. Having been braced for so long, and feeling that first warmer sun, one is caught off guard.

As I was caught February 1960. By Roi's knock at the door. By our starting love. By Merce's dancing, and the magic dark that theatres made that year for the first time as an insistent thing.

As I was caught February 1959. By Zella's embrace in my kitchen, 4 a.m. The thing that moved you finally upstairs.

spring

James and Zen and Bertha. Three of the prettiest people I have ever seen. A fire, the red rug, red lamp, red and gold George Herms painting. All making firelight. James and Zen and Bertha making a party. In a spring-cleaned house. Bertha leaning against the kitchen table, her stomach thrust out, cutting up cheese. In a blue wool dress, her hair done up. Zen with his reddish hair and slow southern speech, sitting next to the heater, watching Bertha's hands. James by the fire loading the wood on, stick by stick. This has been his care since he's been with us. They are waiting for the party to come to the house. They have bought wine. George's show is opening a few blocks away, at the Stryke Gallery, an opening quiet with not enough folly, but George grooving, handing out cups of wine to everyone. Large full canvases of women and children. In sunlight and firelight. This year repeats the last. Even to the date of George's arrival, this year alone, last year with Louise. One or two days difference in the dates. As there were in the dates of the theatre opening. Alan getting sick again, almost to the day. As he did last year. Rash, weariness, depression. This year we are in deeper, there is that. Police come to the house to arrest me for checks. Get talked out of it, but not so easily.

Meanwhile I copyedit Herbert Huncke. That, it took a whole year to bring about, the actual having of the press and shop. A golden yellow place, where I hear your voice. As you pop in the door on the way to class. Where the whir of machine brings lost faces back to me. Lost voices greeting on springwind as I print. Covered with ink, an Italian anarchist's daughter. Or so I should have been. The men who are full of folly have ruled my life. Still do. Grandpa, and you, and Alan. Roi. Great men, full of madness, fill out my vision.

My son is joyous, but sane, too bright to look at. I wait for the dark one's coming. As do you. You live in Alan's study, you and Shiva. I try to hang on to it, hold on to my house. As it slips from my grasp. The prayer of taking refuge chokes in my throat. "My refuge in Shiva and Kali," in the heart, the shell of the whirlwind, the storm rages around us. How I cling to my books, lined neatly on stained wood shelves, my kitchen, my round table, and my friends. Who have been working all these weeks beside me.

The spring, the setting out, year after year. The years I lived in all those furnished rooms—Morton Street, Charles Street, the year I slept in the park. With no possessions but Virgil and laundry tickets. All my clothes I kept in the laundry, one blouse and one pair of slacks on each ticket. Took them out one at a time and put them in. Read Virgil 10 a.m. day after day. Modeled a little to eat, ate out in restaurants. Wandered the city, a good life, the parks and bars. Sitting Sunday afternoons in the Pony Stable Inn, listening to Billie Holliday records and drinking beer. Sitting with Freddie Herko, the bar door open, spring smells floating in.

The room O'Meara and I shared on Morton Street. Trees outside, a luxury, room large, a double bed. Taking home one night Mike Strong, talking three days and nights, the excitement, the giddiness walking by iron rail fences in the dawn, doubled up with laughter. O'Meara going off to live with Mike. Me giving up the room at the end of the week, unable to pay the rent on it alone. Fifteen dollars a week it was, high for those days.

The room I had after that at 70 Charles Street. The shared refrigerator where everyone stole your food. Endless sleepless junkies, whoreladies with dyed red hair. I set out from that room to sleep in the park. Homeless for three months, moving thru summer streets. That was later, after the solstice.

The spring I left home, Lori in town with me. The search day after day for an apartment. The kind of place she'd share. That was February, actually not spring at all. The nights I would go up to New Rochelle to see her. Where she was living with a mad maiden aunt. The night I was up there, posing, she was drawing me, as was Elise, or whatever her aunt's name was, and she told me, ever so cruelly and gently, that she wouldn't come to town to live with me. I stayed quite still, kept posing, a matter of pride. DID NOT BURST INTO TEARS OF FRIGHT AND GRIEF. Did not say but I left school to live with you. Left everything I knew. You must live with me. I said it all that night to my pillow, though, weeping, I seldom have wept thru the whole of a night. As I did then. Next day made a life where I was, what was lost was lost.

Found the first apartment, East Fifth Street, and lived in it. Lori in and out of town, visiting, typing, playing my piano. While I went to work, made monies for both of us.

Now must make a life where I am, what is lost / is lost. How much has been lost these three weeks, next week will tell.

85

This year the setting out has three kids attached. And a husband, mad, but good, who loves me not.

Downstairs they have laid the table for the party. It is finished, everything is ready, Bertha sits by the fire looking into it. Irene has come home from the theatre, no one has come. No one perhaps is coming to this party. It happened this year at Christmas, all Christmas week, no one came to the party, to all the parties. We counted up, we wondered who had been lost. How had they been lost to us. We do not let go so easily, Alan & I.

Last spring for the equinox I went to your house. Early morning it was, it was Sunday, everywhere the Ukrainians had been decking the doors with green branches, whole trees uprooted in some cases. Tillie the vegetable lady was out of everything that grows. "It's a green holiday" she said and that was that. I stopped on the way to your house that Sunday morning and plucked (tore) some leaves off a tree that grew in a lot on Eleventh Street. The tree grew so that its top was just over a fence. I reached up and pulled off three leaves and brought them to you. Up there, where you lived with Deborah. You gave me coffee. Some bread, perhaps, sometimes you had some bread. Some amphetamine, almost certainly, for the day. Always, you were so pleased when I came to visit. And I came often as the spring wore on.

The Hermses were here soon after the equinox. It was partly to get away from the house full of Hermses, Alan, Hermses, confusion, dirt and noise, that I would come up to your house especially on Sundays. Have always

liked visiting people on Sunday mornings in the springtime. Used to drop in on Frank, with a loaf of bread,
onion bread, when he lived on Ninth Street so close to
Tompkins Square… Your house was full of confusion,
but different than mine. Confusion of schmattas, of
which room belonged to whom, confusion of Arione-
ness and Debbie-ness. The blonde woman and the dark.
Confusion of objects. We ate bread, and sometimes
bread and butter. Drank coffee black, sometimes with
sugar or milk. Talked about dancing or writing, gos-
siped about the Hermses. Alan came with me to your
house the day Kirby Doyle arrived. And Kirby said he
had come to fuck you and kill you. That was last spring,
later, Debbie and you insisted Alan said it. That Kirby
had not said anything at all. But he bent over you in the
light, as you lay on the couch. Face down on the couch,
with DeeDee still between you. Hi Kirby, you said, what
are you doing here? And he did say those words, I heard
him say them.

The spring before last spring I was carrying Alex. You
came out to the hills of Topanga Canyon and got me
out of the house. I remember it was springtime but
still chilly and Alan and I were riding home in the MG,
the air rushing by me, Mini in my lap, and I realized
Mini had broken my wedding ring. I searched in the
car for the pearl and found it, but still an ominousness
lay on top of me. The MG pulled into that impossible
angular driveway, and Jeanne who had been left home
ran out to the car. "Mommy, Mommy! Freddie's here!
Freddie's here!" I knew then that in one sense our marriage had ended. Or perhaps that is what is called the
honeymoon. You were very tan and lean, you had been

in Mexico. Had set out on foot thru the jungle when your car died. Michael Malce was with you, he looked like an Indian. His teeth were white when he smiled and he laughed a lot.

After a week you had had enough of seeing Alan and me struggle for survival. You clambered into a station wagon with me and the kids. Left Alan and Billy Linich who'd come out to die, and drove the kids, me, and Michael Malce up the coast. The slowest trip up the coast I ever made. Stopping always to listen to seawind or pick up hitchhikers. Stopping once to smoke pot on the beach and dance on the sand, stoned, while you played your flute and the wind came up. Getting lost once on some incredible dirt road that stopped in a dead end looking at eucalyptus. Huge things towering over the car, we squenched around, turned back, slept in Guadalupe. A one-street town full of pool halls and diners. Mexicans going to work at 5 a.m.

Arrived at San Francisco, at the home of Marilyn Rose (there are no sounds downstairs, no party sounds). Bought food in some quantity for that overflowing house. With Michael Malce's money. Arranged to print my book, *New Handbook of Heaven*. Missed Alan only a little, got stoned a lot. With Kirby Doyle and Lew Welch drunk at that round table. Spewing black metaphors for three days and nights. In this way did they prepare them for their reading. Where they spewed black metaphors without a script. Phil Lamantia screaming in the audience. The goings on in that tower house were many, I had in those days no curiosity. Now, I think I might have found out more about it.

I keep moving backwards, into other springs. That spring with Lori, the long nights in gay bars. The sailor who wept because Joni James was gay. A thing he never expected, being straight. And from Ohio. Last night, in Italian restaurant with Ed Baynard, celebrated spring and remembered him (Joni James was on the jukebox). Remembered also another sailor, same period, same bar (Swing Rendezvous). Said other sailor turned to me after long fruitless time of trying to pick me up, or the girl I was with, someone. Quoth he (dyke with me, named Stevie, had gone off to dance). Quoth he: Do you like girls. Yes, I said, I like girls pretty well. Well, he said, pointing to Stevie, she likes girls and I like girls. Let's go find three girls.

Note to my husband:
I have been split, torn open by our quarrels. Wondering what terrible thing this is, to be a woman. Afraid, I stand my ground. Praying only that you leave me. No sanctuary left me here at all. My horror is endless. I have been paralyzed by it. Help me, undo some of what you have done. I cannot breathe.

Woke up this morning to something of the sense of urgency that used to hold me. A much younger feeling that catapulted me out of bed on Amsterdam Avenue and straight to my Greek, or writing, or whatever. A feeling I had lost, that had been muffled now for years in a kind of desire to be sleepy, to stay half-awake thru most of the doings of the day. Doings that are not my doings, even while I unravel them. But today, sleet falling on my skylight, in the study where I have been sleeping alone, Alan in his study, I woke to that sense that there was a lot to do, all of it beautiful, all of it urgent.

It is not early, but the children are sleeping still, as is Alan, and in the living room on the floor, at least four men. They lie on their sides, on mattresses, mats made of blankets, whatever has come to hand. A Great Dane puppy lies with them. I feel now how it is that here in this tower room I must make the words, the magic that will keep them all safe, that will keep this house around us and give us power. Power to continue. Power of love.

I stop and light incense before my Tibetan relic. The tip of it glows orange, not red I notice. There is on the altar a spring offering. Tangerine Paul Blackburn gave me yesterday, with green leaves and stem. Glowing orange, the highlights of it are made by a candle in red votive glass shining red on the orange skin. And echoed, those highlights, by the orange tip of the incense.

Last night at the theatre did a "happening"—with candles, which Alan dedicated to you. A glorious beehive of making and doing, our city. Into which George dipped his foot for a day or two, then took off. Again to the woods. At my back, in this tower room, the sound of the rain hitting the roof outside, hitting the window. A certain dampness creeps about my ankles. It is the March days, dying. It is as black as the night. My father calls to tell me that we owe him thirty dollars. I think about making some tea, something for breakfast. As the rain gets heavier it hits new keys. It has not started coming thru the skylight yet. Mini creeps up the stairs and comes to visit. I hear her coughing in the hall outside.

Wondering whether or not she should come in. I hear you now, walking in Alan's room. You sit on the edge of the couch and look at him. He sleeps peacefully. He has been exorcised. No demon sits on his forehead this morning. His eyes are clear.

Keep far from us envy, desire, the strong winds
that blow through the human body, scattering it.

I help Mini off with her shirt, remembering one year on Amsterdam Avenue when spring came early, came in January. I was writing a winter story, it never got finished. Finally one warm day in March, looked up at the sky, demanded, with focus of energies, some snow. The sky grew white that day, it snowed for weeks. How angry Joan and Bret were with me, I don't think you noticed at all.

In all those years spring meant you lived by the weather. Days that were clear and warm, one lived outside. Piling the books, and the notebook, on a clipboard, set out with change for breakfast toward Central Park. Stopped at Rudley's on Sixtieth Street right off the park for English muffins and coffee, then went on. Tucked the books away between rocks, went for a ramble. Came back to write, or read, in the sunshine. Dogs, people, children, scrambling up and down. Went back this year to the rocks with the twisted tree, where I used in those days to leave offerings for Apollo. Found now no grass, much dogshit and hard barren ground. Number of people increasing unfathomably. Leaving no room for delights such as I had known them. The privacy of a sunbaked rock, the city, the buildings thrown high all around, like waves breaking on an invisible barrier. Clouds scudding over Central Park South, the towers on the west, the lower and more sedate skyline to the east.

Rambles to the Metropolitan Museum. Hours spent sitting on a sofa that used to be located halfway up the stairs. Paintings above and Egyptian art below. Occasional rambles around looking at things. Mostly one sat and read, or wrote in notebooks. A little bit of art going (even then) a long way.

The reading room at the Whitney, a green, middle-class and comfortable place, was more of a Winter place. As was the reading room at the Donnell Library. In the spring the museums came back into my life. The Met because of the walk across the park being just the right length, and then some hot chocolate at the restaurant by the fountain, and all of that lush beauty to graze and ruminate. The Museum of Modern Art for its garden and small cafeteria looking into the garden. The fact that I always had a pass, scarcely ever missed an old movie they were showing. Marlene Dietrich sitting on a bench in some outdoors in the south, a fallen woman talking to her little boy. The Garbo of *Flesh and the Devil*. Laurel and Hardy. Eisenstein's Cossacks riding thru tenement buildings. Dietrich putting on lipstick at the wall, while the young cadets weep and shoot her. Then back into the sun, a trip to Longley's. More scribbling, and home as it grew dark. To whomever was in the house, and the typewriter. Transcribings and talkings, and suppings there in the night. As the cold crept back to remind us it wasn't summer, and we made fires, slumped in the softening shadows.

I hesitate to go downstairs in my house. Wondering who is still here, who must be got rid of. Wanting the quiet of empty kitchen and bathroom. Thinking I AM NOT A BECK, can't make this scene. But yesterday recovered some of the techniques that I had developed ten, twelve years ago for living with people in droves: e.g., if you want to do anything quiet, go out and do it. Sit in Coscia's for hours, and read your Tibetan sages. Oh, Fred-O, it seems such a stupid thing to say, to think in this black rain, but why aren't you here today to have breakfast with me? So much to tell you of where I am, what has been happening inside my head. I talked to George in the dark two nights ago (he came into the study, night of the opening) and he listened, yes, like a great dark kindly lukewarm pool, but nothing came back, no echoes bouncing off, there is no one knows where I am, except Alan and we are in the same place, no speaking of it. So be it, I can, and I will have breakfast with you. As in my youth I would summon Keats to my side. Or Shelley, for strength or comfort. I take your hand.

I wake each morning in a fallen house. One that has ground to a halt. Ready to take it apart or come away. Alan sleeps on his study couch, he has been to the baths again, the little ground we had cleared for ourselves is gone. Even that. I think back on other springs: were they always thus? Periods of transition, no good at all if you stayed in the house, a time to wander streets, pennies, just pennies, jingling in your pockets… If we cannot go on, we will stop. Simple as that. Send our jade bracelets, unpaid for, back to Trude. I shall get some work to do on my press. We will keep

93

going, fight in court to keep our house. Grimmer, and simpler by far than it has been.

Last spring at this time, the house overflowing with Hermses, all four of them living downstairs. Nalota hiding things under the blankets, biting her sister who crawled around and screamed. Louise secretive, knitting, me inviting her out into the sun. Always the children schlepping along with her. Incredible breakfasts at Coscia's filled with screaming kids. George peaceful almost always, flaring up, striking out at everyone then going back to sleep. Back into himself and painting. Filling up Alan's study. Sparks of love, of happy making-ness flow back and forth over my bookcase from that room to this. I wrote on the last long book. It got dark, and then it got light again. We found a theatre and put ourselves in it. Building a sturdy stage out of whatever: plywood and pipes. Bleecker Street that was, an odd return to the Village. A springtime Village of mounted police and menace. A walled and occupied city.

But that dark room was suspended, was off the earth, spinning its own way to some kind of secret. We crouched in its black walls, in the night, George fashioning something he called a "set," the room began to glow, Alan learned lines. Tried to learn lines. All he had was genius and flair, the other actors became uneasy, fretted about it. I knitted blankets and came to every rehearsal. The room grew huge those hours we spent alone: Alan and George and me, the trips home across an empty city, echoing streets. The stops at Ratner's for coffee, dead fall to sleep. As the weather grew warmer, and Alan got very sick. The air conditioning in that room got louder. The rhythm I beat out between deaths in that play. The night you came there, wandered, lost props, broke things. We were too uptight to take it, sent you away. You never made a dance for that makeshift stage.

And in and around our theatre there was woven that magic dance now mythical, done at the Judson Church on the first of May. "The Palace of the Dragon Prince." Which nobody liked but me, and Alan and Kirby and George. Which New York saw with some astonishment. Since it discarded the precepts of all our teachers. Discarded clean line, exclusion of emotion, became ablaze, and formless, danced in schmattas, old rags and shawls taken from whatever closets. Public manifestation of amphetamine civilization. In which we are all living. "Third Avenue Junkshop Aesthetic" somebody said. Prophetic titles I gave all the pieces. "Oracle for the Brothers." The beauty and grace of your self-abnegation. Confusion and disorder backstage, cloth and chain mail torn to shreds, the whole cast grumbling, but they stuck. Had a feeling something huge was happening. Events were going forward beyond our ken.

Return of the Two-Headed Serpent / Rite of the Five Transits / Dawn of Diminishing Winds / Way of Bright Maze: Hamadryad's Dance – Dance of the Five Faces – Hall of Blue Columns – Ring of Dark Mist / Oracle for the Brothers / Slope of Fire (Zenith) / Slope of Fire (Nadir) / White Forest Dance / Night Litany: Pavanne for the Widows – Word of the White Cat – Pause for Jade – Point of Deepening / Black Wine Uncovered / Five Transits Concluded.

I am glad that this gift, at least, I made without stinting.

These titles, glinting like jewels. Jeanne sitting at the feet of the Dragon Prince. Alan and I in full costume, cape and gown, we came as we were. The outer mode and the inner knowledge met, what you paid for with your death.

Two days later saw Remy Charlip in Coscia's. Asked him how he had liked your dance. "I thought it was appalling, just appalling," said Remy Charlip. And he was right, it was.

There was some sun this morning, it glinted in thru the skylight onto my bed. If there had not been this sun, I am sure I would be sleeping still, there is a heavy hand on each of my shoulders, pressing me down, to chair, or floor or bed. But the sun drew me up by the hair, and led me to you. The sun has already "gone in," the sky is clouded. I hear the beginnings of rain on the skylight now.

April 2. It seems that we are setting out again, Alan and I and the children. Having made that theatre, red satin, a place for you, we are leaving it. It is not a place for us. And you are not here to fill it. It has been snowing even in April, then raining, the roof outside is wet, Alan sleeps on my couch in this room, the typing doesn't seem to bother him. We have come together, very close, in the midst of "calamities." As they may be called. As they would be considered by the outside world. Phones being cut off. No money at all. All our theatre staff rebelling and going away. As well they might. Two puppies, unhousebroken, roaming the lower floor. I look at my books, wonder what to leave behind me. What to sell. Not much. I think about getting offset plates made in "the country," wonder a lot how it will all turn out.

The panorama of other springs flashes by me. The spring when Jeanne was a baby, no trouble at all, just the one child, a part of me. Wheeling her to the Village, to the park. Where I would sit in the sun, with her in my lap. Reading, or scribbling (still) in notebooks among the new green. There is no new green yet this year, and that is strange. No yellow green on trees, or on the ground. I remember how late the leaves were, falling last autumn. They would not fall till you had. And wonder what the new grass is waiting for...

Angus just appeared on the stairs—the wanderer—and little dark Piero, smiling sadly. I do love Angus. He gave me a terrible brilliant lithograph out of India, and wandered off again. When I said I was writing. Talking to Angus is like being half awake and it begins to rain. Talking to Piero is like dealing with the outside world. I fled back to the study. Mini was crying somewhere below down there.

As you left then, or tried to, we leave now. As you would have left for Mexico, if you could have. Nobody here will regret our going at all. Read prayers on Wednesday nights to a changing crowd. No friends but Audre and Mo. Jimmy has turned into the thing he was becoming in the last days of your earthlife. When he denied you the use of his studio. I wonder how I will transport the altar you made me. Decide I'll have to ride the whole way with it on my lap.

Other springs: the spring I spent with Zella. In her apartment on Seventeenth Street, in a building that had once been a stable. Lovely top floor, gabled windows, great white walls. Inside of which we lingered, Zella absorbed. I sometimes impatient, wanting to get out. The concerts, the dances, the readings we kept on missing. As we made love on that bed. My vague ennui. The taste of that little park on Seventeenth Street. In the spring rain, night after night, walking Zella's dog. "Nails" was his name, an ugly, too-fat boxer. Remember one morning walking that dog at dawn. It was raining, that fat flat brown Episcopal church stood guard over the greening park in the spring rain. A man on a bench was sitting, huddled over. He'd breathe, one great rasping breath, and there'd be a pause. Quite a long pause. And then he'd do it again. Went home with Nails, breakfasted, slept, worked the day thru. That night well after twilight returned to that park. The rain still fell, the man still slumped on the bench. He breathed no better, he probably died in the night.

Returned last Sunday to that park with Alan. Who was still absorbed in all kinds corporate structures. The puppy, Pasha, romped, the church looked down. The air was clear, cool, joyous. Children were playing. Alan's hands were shaking, he trembled with the cold. We have returned since then to our own ways.

The light is changing. The day is becoming darker. I shall go to Coscia's for coffee, and buy some milk for the children. I shall call a rehearsal of the last two plays we'll be doing. At least for a while. I shall call up our creditors and hold them off. I shall clean the study, and get Alan up. The day will bumble along, tonight we will do

98

something—plays or whatever. Alan & Jeanne & I will improvise. Wrapped in my bedspread, Alan looks like a purple mummy. Echoes of children and animals from downstairs. Bertha goes off to get bread and her own apartment. Our cupboard is barer than it has ever been. The I Ching has given us "Darkening of the Light." Over and over again in the past two weeks.

I hear your castanets, your bracelets on the stairs, your loud, demanding voice, waking up the house. As you throw your ruana back over one shoulder, stirring the air. I only wish there were birds outside the window.

Looking back on it now, I wonder was there more I could have done. To keep the theatre open, or whatever. Had that champagne party for the second opening. Not assumed so many other people knew what they were doing (they didn't). They didn't at all. As all around me people said that I must relegate more of the responsibility, not worry so much about it, let others do it, should I have even then taken that as a warning, a clear sign to do the opposite, to check into every move Irene made, every plate Zen pasted, whatever? Never to have given back the reins to Alan when he returned ranting from California— would that have salvaged it, or part of it? Ifs, ifs, grey, line up on both sides of my life, like on both sides of a road, and I walk through them. No doubt, the road we have taken is the road we should take. "What you depart from is not the way," I remember. Always this squeezing by, this skin of our teeth life. I remember absurdly enough one spring morning on East Houston Street, the man who had a building two buildings away decided to recoat his brick wall with tar, not let in the rain, etc. Men on scaffoldings worked away in the morning air. Anna next door threw them a pulley and a rope, and they fastened a clothesline where none had ever been (our anxiety to have always more clotheslines was unequalled since the days of Vasco da Gama). Days later, landlord looked up at his newly tarred wall, and had apoplexy. How did she get that clothesline into my wall? "The birds, she has the birds even working for her!"

Zip. Zip. Rip. Off it comes. Another layer.

Dear Freddie:
I am closing the circle, last night I performed at that red satin theatre we made you. Tonight again in three plays this time, all three on the program. I am bringing it all my newfound corniness, it is "appalling" I am sure. Jerry Benjamin has made something consummately dull out of Poet's Vaudeville. Not too bad to look at, but quite dull to perform. No action. I plan to liven it up tonight. The excitement in this, an old excitement, no new tastes, that's the point, what I meant to write you about. No new tastes in this either, I am waiting. To stop repeating myself. I repeat myself, only better than last year, but that is small comfort at this point. My head is whirling, it is April but very cold. The brilliant sun, two dogs I do not like much. No new tastes. We will buy this house, or we will move away. Perhaps then in the making of a house, one of my chiefest pleasures, it will be as if I act, not as if I remember. I don't know. So far remembering has been all of it. George arrived to the date, same time this year as last. We opened our theatre, same time this year as last. Only thing is, we're holding out a little longer. The Blossom,

*if we do it again, will be going on this year same date as
last year. Like playing a loop of tape, over and over. The
volume is varied slightly, is all.*

   Diane

A picture of Alex Giallo stares at me, out of a box of
Freddie's things. One of the dozens of boys who sat on
my couch and told me how much they were in love with
Freddie. Spring after spring after spring. On that dumpy
foam rubber couch, in my living room, asking questions. Why Freddie never really unfolded to them. The
simple answer: he was not in love with them, I softened
in various ways from year to year. Alex was one of the
simplest to answer, cooler and wiser than most. Alex
I met again, the night before Freddie died. On a dark
and echoing street where I walked with Alan. When we
should have been at the party on Ridge Street, long before, party Freddie was making, but we had lingered at
Bret's house. It was twelve, or later, the streets were deserted and ominous. We talked with Alex of how they
were ominous. He asked how Freddie was, we tried to
tell him. Flippant about it all. And then proceeded. At
Second Avenue found it was 1 a.m. Too late for any
party. We went home.

Peter Hartman was one for whom the answer was
complicated. That Freddie was bored eternally with
him. Peter took refuge downstairs, we spoke mythologies. We sniffed cocaine together, Peter buying. Peter
set out for India, to study. Returned in two months,
tanned and older, moved in with me. We set out to get
married, but we failed. Roi too much lingering about

101

the place. The smells of him still on the sofa. Peter set out for the Virgin Islands, the Village, Rome, where he still is, he called on the day of Freddie's funeral. We are not broken, love stretches fine between us. Although he used to lie on the bed in my house and listen to the noises upstairs at Freddie's. Wracked and tortured and adolescent (he turned twenty-one the year we didn't get married)... One day on Fourth Street, a few years after that, one sunny day in February, Jeanne drew a circle on the floor, and told Peter and me to stand inside it. We did. She told us that the circle was full of fire, and that when we came out of it we would be new, like "babies." We did. We were. We were to do so again some days later to confirm our state of newness. I don't believe we kept the second appointment.

Two photos under Alex sits Arione. In Paris now, on her way to India. Where we shall meet, all of us, I am sure, again. "We shall pass each other in saffron robes and bow." Was what I told Kirby Doyle.

It is definitely spring. I have just turned down the heater. At Coscia's wanted nothing but tea and brioche. No more egg sandwiches, to help me hold out in the cold. It is definitely spring, and we are closing the theatre.

At Coscia's this morning the echo of other springtimes. The days when I lived with you at Joan O'Meara's, 32 East Seventh Street, all our possessions in dresser drawers on the floor. Taking turns sleeping in the bed, which was small and uncomfortable. Watching the bedbugs at dawn stroll to and fro. The Second Avenue Griddle where we would go for waffles and bacon. My terrible trips to work at an insurance office in the Village. Where I would meet Mo for lunch, amid the packing of meat on Ninth Avenue. Me pregnant with Jeanne, my stomach too big for lunch counters.

The springs before that, wandering the Village. The sleeping in Washington Square, and getting up to Virgil, to the writing. Those notebooks not so interesting now, looking back. How I kept my clothes in twos in the Chinese laundry, one pair of slacks, and one shirt on each ticket, is interesting still. I would get one outfit out (clean underwear in the ballet bag I took with me everywhere) change in Rienzi's john, or one of the apartments I had the key to, and bring the dirty ones in, another ticket. How the park attendants would wake us at six by sweeping, and then I would fall back asleep till ten or so. When the sun got strong, and the people started to arrive. I would get up then and begin my day. Coffee at one of those espresso houses full of old men playing pinochle at that hour, and a walk, sometimes to the library, then to the park and to Virgil, and later to model. Meet O'Meara in the afternoon and talk a lot. Sitting in some bar or coffee shop writing in notebooks.

The day that bum bought me a bowl of soup. "Brown eyes, you look like you need something to eat." Propelling me into a greasy spoon on Third Avenue. Pea soup 15¢, we both sat down to a bowl. "Brown eyes, do you know I was born outside of time?" "Lord Byron was a son-of-a-bitch, was he not, brown eyes?" "If I tell you something, I can never get it back. Do you know anything about time and space?"

103

Echoing, last spring, the bum of Third Avenue, in front of Cooper Square as I left the house. He came to me and earnestly grasped my hand. "Believe the news they never teach you. Believe the news they never teach you." I said OK, and he said "And take care of your sister."

The light has changed, is softer, soon there will be the smell of vegetation. The grocer on Sixth Street looks sadly at the pavement, and tells me it's the time now to plant vegetables. Forty years in the city, he still thinks of the softening earth.

First spring I knew you, before we lived together, you wanted to take Joan O'Meara to hear Myra Hess (being as you told me years later, in love with Joan, and afraid of tough dyke me in leather jacket who went with her everywhere). She in her usual insouciance was late, you waited till the concert had well begun, then left the ticket for her and went in. I still remember how disturbed you were later, how touching your disturbance that she had not come. In Westchester, I guess, you were handsome and run after. Not used to being stood up.

The spring I spent mostly with Zella on Seventh Street. Leaving you to watch Jeanne on Houston, those strange sleepless nights. While I strode about the chaos of that girl's life, drinking coffee at Frankie & Charlie's on Fourth Street and Avenue C, or going to Johnny Miller's, open all night, where a waitress named Ruthie chatted endlessly. I remember in the slow long nights of that strange summer (1959) sitting at Frankie and Charlie's one night while the local whores & hoods had a napkin fight. Rolled up balls of paper napkins flew back and forth, and every one took cover under tables, and behind counters for a full half hour.

The sadness that came on Saturday with this soft weather. On Saturday afternoon while Alan napped. I sat in here and tasted this spring to the full. Tasted the fact that you would return no more. That unquestionably youth was past, and thoughtlessness. Easy days. Heard my children growing up around me. That night did the plays for you, did them brilliantly. In a vacuum, where no one took delight in the hasty, impromptu nature of the evening. Tried calling Debbie, thought at least it would amuse her, my learning the part at eight, going on at nine. But no Debbie at home, she lives now in another world. Quite beyond anything I know anything about. No one left but Alan & I who know that plays are play were playing, that playing itself is sacred. Performed brilliantly in a vacuum, had blessed dreams.

Jeanne too that night dreamed well, dreamed you taught her in a school where all the children jumped off the roofs and nothing happened to them (they floated about).

Was it not spring too when you lived on Prince Street. You dwelt there with a long, sad boy with a crooked nose. Named Eddie Johnson. There were at least two Eddie Johnsons. Eddie Johnson was in love with you as I found out one night, when Allen G. & Peter & Jack Kerouac came over, and stayed, and we pushed all the beds together. Eddie lay there crying in my arms while you were screwing Allen. Saw him not long ago, from a Fifth Avenue bus. He was all suited and tied, he works someplace uptown. How sad it is for them, for all of them. The gay boys, growing older, the old dreams dead. They do it so many times, over and over again. The same bright color, the same change to greys. No staying power in it. Why Cocteau is a saint, he held to it.

Prince Street was our first loft, ever, lofts were rarer then, I don't know if that's what we called them, even. Fireplaces, partitions, a bathroom downstairs, that was shared with the boy who had the loft beneath. Green plants and growing things. In all the houses that were ever yours (this was the first, as Amsterdam Avenue was mine) you had green plants aplenty. I remember now that when I went to Eleventh Street with Debbie to clean out everything, two days after you died, there was an avocado plant growing in the front room. Thin, tenuous, it had held on somehow in the soot. I thought of taking it back to Cooper Square with me, but plants always die when I have them. I forget to water them, or give them too much sun, or not enough, I simply never manage it so they survive, and I couldn't bear the thought of watching that avocado fade & die, so left it there to die out of my sight, telling myself maybe someone would come and take it. (We left the door open, people came and stayed. People came and took whatever loot was left. Huncke slept there a while, and Joel Markman.)

The kitchen at Prince Street always was a mess. No one ever washed the pots, we were too busy. You were always rushing late to ballet theatre, after some parched scrambled eggs cooked in all that confusion and eaten out of the pan, or a dirty plate. You always managed to make the eggs stick to the pan. Cooked them too hot, my life with you was a succession of dirty frying pans with dried up eggs in them.

From there to O'Meara's, and from O'Meara's to Vincent's. By then it was summer.

Next spring I had Jeanne, we were living on Houston Street. You were working at Equitable Life Insurance, you had a Black friend named Doris Blount, and we turned on a lot in the evenings. I remember the second or third time we got high together, finding you at the far end of that L-shaped apartment, on the threshold of the study, wrapped around the door frame which you were embracing passionately and weeping. A few minutes later, still weeping, and looking rueful, you came back into the living room to say "First time in my life I ever fell in love, and it had to be with a door jamb."

Next spring found you upstairs and me with Roi. Was Eddie Royce with you? I think so. Dear Eddie, a dark Sagittarius, cuddly but hard to handle. I used to come up for coffee in the morning. I had a 104 fever, on and off. And a purple inside to my mouth, it had been painted with gentian violet by a not too smart doctor because it was covered with sores. Later all diagnosed as mononucleosis. Roi has it still. We screwed thru fever dreams in the April air. Anna next door sending food over on the clothesline. The other neighbors shocked beyond belief at the carryings on. Jeanne getting older and wiser very fast.

"Jeanne" said Roi, "do you want to learn to fly?"
"No" said Jeanne, "I want to stay in the sunshine."
"Don't people fly in the sunshine?"
"No, they stay in the house and fly."

The plays at the Living Theatre, and a concert that included *Extravaganza*. I stage-managed a lot, the plays were full of props.

By that May I'd had enough of Roi, and fled away. To a sad & dumpy house at Greenwood Lake, where I wrote and wrote and discovered I was pregnant.

HOW I BECAME DISGUSTED WITH ROI AND LEARNED ABOUT KARMA. A Legend.

That spring, there were many comings and goings from my house to a house on West Twentieth Street, off Tenth Avenue, where the Joneses lived. Many a day I would spend at that house with Jeanne, and many a day (Wednesday) I would leave Jeanne there and go to the museum, to the 5:30 movie, where I would meet Roi, who worked in the neighborhood. Hettie would have gone earlier to the 3 p.m. showing, while I watched Keli, who was still a babe in arms. Roi and I would meet and movie, (sometimes with one of his other chicks, too) and then return in the gathering dusk of that springtime to Tenth Avenue and Twentieth Street. That house had a certain magic. The front room, large, had a blue-tiled fireplace, a good phonograph, a comfortable couch, and ghosts. Ghosts stalked the whole three front rooms of the place, I remember how often I caught them with the corner of my eye, leaving or entering those sunny rooms.

Often I would stay for supper, and on into the evening, Jeanne falling asleep on Roi & Hettie's bed, Keli always rocked to sleep, never allowed to cry, even a little. After supper Roi would turn on, and work, reading manuscripts and typing, and Hettie and I would work on the Totem Press books, pasting and typing up Philip Whalen or Ron Loewinsohn. So the time went by until one evening Hettie told me she wanted to talk to me. I went with her into Roi's study, Roi in the front room with the young men was listening to a new jazz record. And she said "I know you and Roi have been making it for some time." I was taken aback and thought for a moment of denying the whole thing, but that seemed somehow foolish and cheap and so I said nothing and waited for her to continue. "I don't mind," she said, "but Roi has got to understand that I need some freedom too. I have been seeing Mike Kanemitsu." This I knew, Hettie and I had had many long confidential talks, although until tonight she was the only one with confidences to impart, I felt that I simply could not tell her that I was sleeping with her husband. She had had an affair with Alfred Leslie, for a while thought she was pregnant by him, and then had taken up with Mike Kanemitsu, another painter in our set. She went on to say that she was tired of lying and sneaking, that she hoped that if I talked to Roi he would understand that she was simply doing what she had to do, and that they could live together as man and wife if he could be understanding as she was of his affair with me. I told her I would try to talk to him that night.

After a while I left with Roi for the Five Spot. Stopped on the way at the Artists' Club where there was a party in progress, with a message for Mike from Hettie. The message was simply that Hettie had to speak to him, but it catapulted him right out of the dance he was doing with three chicks, and right out of the Artists' Club to a phone, so I gathered he was hung up on her too and was glad.

We stayed at the Five Spot a while and drank a little. I think Ornette was there, it was very crowded. Finally, Roi and I set out for my place as we had so many nights. I gave it to him straight from the shoulder, and he took it badly, muttering about middle-class morality (Hettie's) which I thought was rather a turnabout and still do. Told him Hettie was doing no more than what she ought, if she were to be able to stand to live with him. Nothing came thru, so finally I just unclenched one of his fists and asked him "can you be angry in bed?" and got him there, into that large kind bed where we'd been on so many trips. Made love till almost dawn, then Roi, donning his shoes and his anger, set out. I too was angry by then, told him to wait for the daylight, to sleep beside me, having slept with me, but no, he was off.

The rest is heresay. How he arrived at his house and found no Hettie, which was what he had expected. A.B. and Joel were there, and tried to cool it. How he went to Mike Kanemitsu's and dragged her home. How he went home and broke every dish in the house. Then went back to Mike's, planning to kill him, and Mike greeted him civilly and offered him coffee or beer (it was then about 6 a.m.). Roi told me later that he wandered the streets then for hours not sure whether or not he had killed Mike.

110

By that evening, he and Hettie had made up. Perhaps this proved to her that he loved her, I don't know. Told him that night that he was in love with Hettie, or anyway that they had to make it somehow. That I was getting out, was going away. Not to see them again for a while, not to see him as we were ever again. "If it means that much to you, and it obviously does, then work at it."

Felt that the whole thing was just too uncivilized. Roi most of all. Could never understand how, behaving as he did, and he was sleeping with a great many people, of both sexes, he would allow no leeway for anyone else. At Greenwood Lake I was sad, but relieved, heavy with loneliness, yet feeling clean somehow and as if I had gotten back on a right track. Dharma I was discovering existed. Then one day it began to dawn on me that I was pregnant. That I had gotten pregnant the night of all that anger. Slow horror, and my return to New York, and an abortion. Karma, I discovered, existed too.

The abortion, a mutual crime, bound me and Roi together for two more years.

April 6. So Alan has left as he always leaves in the spring, I remember that he left you once in the spring, and your subsequent chagrin, and shame, and sorrow. How you swore that you could not have him back. How you had him back, and how he left again, this time more or less for good. How sad you were, how you wept for days on my couch, that same foam rubber couch, rank and covered with stains. How I would wake in the night, and say "Freddie dear, take another sleeping pill" trying to mask my annoyance at being woken by your tears, your endless sobs. Which eventually, after a few weeks, left you, and left you high and dry, another creature. Never to be the same creature again. And now Alan has left me he has gone off with his two large dogs to Scranton Pennsylvania where he will be met by his father and then shown farms. If we can sit writing books and growing calves who at the ripe old age of ten weeks will be slaughtered. A non-Buddhist occupation, but lucrative. He is tired of hassling, I am tired of hassling. One gets very tired of hassling in the spring.

I have asked him if possible not to come back till May Day. I am feeling again the stretch and spaces of my life. The ennui of being able to write all day. The sudden panics: nothing to say at all, why am I writing. I cannot get thru the boredom of retyping THAT. Whatever. It is a great peace and joy, this kind of boredom. The rows of books stretched out. New notebooks filling, old ones resuscitated. I push and push against the lack of funds (Alan never goes till the last of the money is spent). Desire to mail out *Bears*, and print some more. Desire to get the plates made for A.B.'s book. Have dreadful fears of running out of good paper: Sphinx Esquire Bond, 20 lb., is the kind I use. The mail today brought no money, which was strange. First time in weeks. All signs say it's run out.

No longer love as I used to take long walks. To strut about the landscape, drinking coffee. Bearing notebooks under one arm, in all kinds of weathers. Only to pray, to study, to write and read. Came today upon letters written in 1961. One on March 22 to Peter Hartman in Africk. All about someone called Irwin who with a claymore (!) cut off the head of a naked statue (male) belonging to one, Byrne Fone. Who fancied himself in love with said Irwin. Who in turn fancied himself straight. All this happened long ago in other springs, in a house we planned to make into a musical called "Tenement." Remember? We never did it. Remember the building united to eject Irwin: two dykes Zella & Alice in the pad next door, moved things about for hours, the boys upstairs made quite a clatter and racket. Marlene & Bill, two of the saddest people in the world, lived right over Byrne & came down with Freudian comments. Irwin threw the beheaded statue into the street. Houston Street was covered with white plaster dust. Zella's dog was very excited, as I recall.

Herbert Huncke came here this morning and had some tea. Waiting for the sandal shop to open, so he could sell some acid and buy his fix. Sleepy and polite, having been up all night. His clothes smelled of spring dawns, as George's used to after his walks to the river.

But I must admit it, I am tired. Tired of the endless hassle to keep things going. How many landlords have pounded on my door, over the years, each one angrier than the last? How many last quarters doled out for quarts of milk? Cans of mushroom soup for Jeanne and Mini. Poor-food. Should I buy stamps today, or orange juice? Typing paper, or ink for the press? Etc. And now the endless hassle with the theatre, what plays go on this weekend, Helen Adam wants one night off to go to the Hardware Poets Theatre. Jerry Benjamin won't repeat his *Poet's Vaudeville*. Etc. Throw together another happening, learn more lines. Alan is off in Pennsylvania. I cannot follow you. I would if I could. Alan, too, would, I know. I have seen that in him that the game itself is a scramble, and wrong for us. Not sure I can anymore play it. Three months rent due at the store where the press is, one month at the theatre, bills on four telephones… And Sunday night no audience at all. Was reminded of your party on Ridge Street roof. Thought "People know when to stay away, an animal instinct." Well, perhaps it is just that the sun isn't out today. That I got out of bed and tripped over an extra mattress, smashing my ribs and hip. That things cannot be hurried, whatever I do. It will be this evening before I negotiate the check we got last night. For one of George's pieces. It will be tomorrow before I buy typing paper. Next week I will run A.B.'s book, not this week as I'd planned. If we can hang on till Dali's happening, I may give the landlord the option money on this house. Or have it to give him if Alan hates life in the country. The children are happy, there are oranges. They shout at the oranges, and at each other. People shout at the door, I let them in, send them off to make offset plates and cash dubious checks. There are to be films tonight at the theatre, but nothing yet has been done about them at all. I call Andy Warhol's studio, covered as it is with tinfoil, the place where you spent the last night of your life riding up & down in the elevator, and get Billy Linich on the phone. He sounds well. He knows nothing. Nobody knows hardly nothing anymore. That's how it is and has been. I'll make A.B.'s book since I have the paper for that. It has turned cold again, damp as well as sunless. As if it forgot that it was supposed to be spring. Another fall. Walked Mini home from nursery school, walked slowly, not hurrying as I usually do with the stroller. Grey streets, and poverty everywhere like Mexico. A man was cementing the front of a crumbling house. Shoring up. Doing his best to make it do a while. A seven year old child walked by with a pacifier in her mouth, she looked contented. They all had shoes of some kind, tho hardly any of them fit. Poverty, but not extreme. Bad enough. My shoes are new. If it had not been that I lost the last button off my Winter coat, only yesterday at that, just in the nick of time, I would have felt like an American tourist. To be hooted at and robbed. Crossing Avenue B like crossing the border from El Paso into Juarez. The crumbling front of the Mobilization for Youth building. The obscenities written out front. The flag wasn't even up in front of that overcrowded school on Fourth Street, between C and D. I wondered idly if we'd seceded during the night. While I slept, my dreams full of the jazz that had been at the theatre. The night before. Large shades, all drunk or stoned, wandered in & out. LeRoi, looking younger and happier for the music... Marion Brown, the Wanderer, gentle soul, played a sweet sad solo, twenty minutes of it. I go it blind. My window today is grey & my skylight is grey. The Book told me "possession in great measure."

So the days proceed, without dogs or calamities. As the children and cats get happier in the house. More certain of their place, their size and survival. The smell of dogs-hit leaves the hallway. The bills can be taken up, one at a time, and examined. And paid, or forgotten. As the air settles down, around and under our shoulders.

115

This morning on the way to the bank, came down the subway stairs as an F train pulled in. Same train, same cars, I am sure, that I used to ride from Brooklyn on my way to Hunter High School. They even smelled the same. The rush and space of those mornings and that sadness, so much the same as the sadness of now, as if I knew then all these years between, and the sorrow in them and the horror. I see that now in Jeanne's eyes when I wake her for school. The infinite grief of her lifetime stretching before her. All to be tasted now, immediate. And I thought, again, as I got onto the car, that I had closed some circle. That they were closing (snap) one by one behind me, the circles. And wondered objectively if I had long to live. "Not if I have to live like this" I thought. Whatever that might mean. But it had something to do with dogshit and feeling crowded, and wet noses poking at me in the morning, and Alan more frivolous, more a gay young thing. As he gets older, and his life gets harder. Crazier than ever, more and more the con man. A weight my life won't support. As you were, before you died, an object that would not float. Not even buoyed up by his hair, tho it falls to his shoulders.

SHE SHOULD NOT FOLLOW HER WHIMS.
SHE MUST ATTEND WITHIN TO THE FOOD.
PERSEVERANCE BRINGS GOOD FORTUNE.

So the Book sets me straight again. I shall go to the doctor, and have my glands restored to the proper size and function. I shall sit at this typewriter many mornings, remembering other springs: N.B., NO BITCHING. OK.

No! Enough of this! I am stifling. It must change! I will not look timidly at my dreams and look away. I must laugh more. I will hear more music. There is a shell that is atrophied about me, let it crack! As the surface of the earth cracks, ceaselessly, it is spring. O beloved, stay away, stay away for weeks! Till the air in the house is changed, and I put out / new leaves.

Decision Day—two dogs barking next door & the incursion of so many other springs, echoing, the rides to school in the subway, leaning against businessmen with hardons, for balance, while I wrote out my Latin translations. The echoing tunnels at Grand Central Station. Flowers all winter in those stands, candy bars, carnivals of failure. The stand I am learning to take is quite different from any that I have taken before. Last night in my dream, leaning against an old lover with a hardon, the word UNFORESEEN blazoning across the picture. That Events Unforeseen were going to happen to us. Big Ray Johnson beaming at both of us. Half prophecy, half omen.

Letter to Alan: Husband, it will take me about six months to finish off what must happen in the city. If you can leave me here till December—alone, I will get straight by then be ready to join you. your loving,

Wyfe

Trying to picture the farmhouse we maybe go to, I sit here, having just returned from the markets of Ninth Avenue, "Russian, Greek, Italian Specialties" hanging on racks. The marketplace of a great city, soon to vanish. The heaps of twisted mortar on this spot. Where no city was before, and none will ever grow again. Manahatta. Great rock, once 70 miles from shore, and white with bird droppings. Great rock, now the ravaged earth lets go of you, as we shall let go / let the earth / drop from our fingers.

But not without songs, and rejoicings. I see the new people, they are hairier than the old. They are wreathed in perpetual, goony, elaborate grins. They are fatter and skinnier than their ancestors. They are bigger and speak more slowly. They dance almost all the time, they play flutes, one note for days, the devas are visible to them, they converse with dakinis and comfort the hungry ghosts. That which we did with pain, and terror and guilt, the dancing in sidestreets at midnight to the moon, the loading platforms used for impromptu stages, and long harvest dances in the Swing Rendezvous, to Dinah Washington's rhythm and blues on the jukebox, these things are now won, they are rights, the young can do all this without anger, without belligerence. The love that we brought to birth in sadness and sorrow / is lighting up the air. (It will light up the air thru the orange flash, thru the infinite thunderbolt of the great war) and wash us like gentle waves onto new shores. Our work is done, the young men wear their hair to their shoulders, the babies are dirty and caper in the streets, the young women dance, they are openly sexual. I shall take my place with the old ones of this tribe. Rear the babies, and tell stories, all the stories I can remember. Kirby & I shoring up mythologies. Our work is done. Some of us died, I know, in the doing of it. And some of us will die because it is done. Unable to take our place in the new order, in the slowness and understatement of that air. Now that the high excitement and style of battle / falls from our shoulders like gold & silver capes.

Some shall take their places as the old ones of this tribe. To bring highlights into the colors the young girls wear. To teach the young men proud words, they walk so soft. But they have discovered who they are. And meet as gods, gracious in luminous air. Ambiance. Condescending to this earthtime and this place. The grins getting larger as they caper like children. John, I fear we are the only discordance here, in this new world we have fashioned, or paved the way for. Too stern we are, involved with flamboyance and praise. High words of fame. The stars dance for them like lights of hallucination. There are no swords, no ploughshares. Roi, Kirby, Alan, perhaps we are the discords. Freddie felt this, and removed himself. But they must hear our songs, commit them to memory, or the earth will go flat. I wonder about this sometimes. All those flutes, and as yet no musicians... But perhaps it takes five hundred years before the musicians emerge. Bob Creeley, you are an arrogance on the earth. Fierce brightness. "But a tawdry cheapness / shall outlast our days." But the children sing, the young people smile a lot.

And Christopher Marlowe went mad, and Pound went mad. And Christopher Smart, and Allen Ginsberg, and Proust. (Though no one called it madness.) And the earth is trembling with the weight of the thing it carries. It quivers with twinges and pangs of the weeks before labor. The Christ and the Buddha were nothing to the glory / that shall burst on us now.

119

GOOD FRIDAY, 1965

1. She rises and bathes

10:30 a.m. & the sun has gone in already. It was
so bright this morning.
Perhaps we'll never have more than two hours of
    sunshine
at a time, again. Johnny Dodd says
he thinks that soon all the animals will die
as the birds are dying.
I reminded him the buffalo are breeding
in Canada, but now I wonder about it. The silence:
all those animals gone & the jungles
"defoliated." New times demand new words.

Last night we stripped the theatre of lights & props
"defoliated" and passed them on to another
theatre, which will go on. I'm not sure what we'll do
we will go on, we will read
in that stripped-down theatre, for three days & nights

I will return the jewels we bought, strip down
again, and the dogs
(we paid for neither)
you will come home.
You will get ready to go to India.

Downstairs a last child is crying, not my child
I sent mine away, last night, for three days & nights
the silence
echoed strangely at dawn

The heater goes on & off, I write this poem
I think of the ones who are gone & the ones who are here
this is sad rejoicing, *christos vos*— how do you spell it?
outside the world turns green—for the last time?
Soon it will strip.
There will be nothing left but the letters of that mantra
Tibetan block letters: OM MANI PADME HUM
arching over our heads, and dancing under our feet
while we walk, transparent, aircolored inbetween
like in old diagrams I have seen in books.

I think of you, Freddie, playing "Caladonia"
in that saffron dress & white headband
defoliating, stripping down to bone
in the soggy eastcoast earth.
An earth I sometimes think breeds only decadence
(Gerry Malanga in black satin dress
or the face of Piero Heliczer at the theatre)
resplendent flesh. Something indescribably soft
& maggoty about it. As if it would drop away
(like ripe plums)
at a look or touch
leaving only bones, or seed.

(the seeds blew over the earth when we buried you
the ground must be soft green now
that soft air
in which one can feel the turning of the earth
the tilting of the river toward the sky...)

I think of Kirby playing his clarinet
in the woods outside of Berkeley, where the ocean
lifts up, and toward the sun, I think of George

most decadent of us all, on Topanga hills,
will they rise again? for you it is easy
"when's Freddie" asked Mini "gonna come out of that
    dying"

2. She returns from a walk

Has *Lunch Poems* come out yet at the 8th Street
    Bookstore?
I wonder about that—I'd like to read them all
on the roof in the sun (it has
come out again)
Picture of Vincent Warren last night at Jimmy's
the classical ballet dancer
that elegance & fierce innocence
an anomaly—how did that ever
come out of Tallahassee? No wonder
Frank fell in love with it.

Frankie Francine is pounding at the door
he wants to come in & get his things
all of which have long since been looted & thrown away
He sees his suitcases all neatly stacked and ready
packed with shoplifted underwear different sizes
mother of pearl cufflinks
costume jewelry
as I see dismembered Dionysius in the earth: the limbs
painfully knitting together, underground
or the sky darkening & the graves
giving up their dead…
the sun has come out again, perhaps after all
the animals will live.

3. She goes to the roof to meditate

All things on earth have slipped away from me
the gulf between this year & the one before
the last time I came to this roof to read Milarepa
the children were made of flesh & blood, I was certain
that there were duties that I had to do.
that there was work for Alan and for me.
that there were friends who loved us.

Now I sit alone in the sun on some kind of peak
the waters do not reach; I watch the veil
sunbleached & rainsoaked it falls to tatters
before the strengthening winds.
Sunbleached & rainsoaked, I see thru the threads
sunyata, the void, and my original face
the eyes of that face swallow me: I am free
I move my hands like stars above the ground

All things on earth are remembering what they were.
Roofs rise like rocks, the traffic sounds of the sea.
Women flock to the laundromat on their way
to the river, with their sheets, they have that look
The shapes are eternal, our vision
had grown obscure.

4. She continues to meditate

This is not my house anymore: I have no house
I live in it like one who passes through
They are not my children: Mini may go to Roi
Jeanne may leave for the west, and Alexander

must go to the monastery when he is twelve.
And Alan must set out on a terrible journey
I pray will bring him closer to his peace.
Defoliating. I am becoming light.
My bones shine thru my flesh. It falls away.

5. She returns the child to its mother

Haven't walked thru the streets like this, carrying a
    baby
since my first one. Later, one holding your skirt
& one in your arms: that gets to be too much, it slows
    you down
You leave them home. I do.
On Fourth Street they take a radio apart
releasing (stripping) "a perfectly good speaker"
from plastic.
Talk over it in Spanish.
Defoliating.
There is dust in my eyes.
The wind is high.
Streamers are blowing like prayer banners
off the streetlights.
I buy some ink & wool & return to the house.

6. She leaves for the theatre at 3 p.m. exactly

Has the sky darkened? Has the earth
torn asunder? No, in fact
the sun has come out again.
The city magic & simple, as any place is

When you are alone in it and a little stoned.

7. She returns from the theatre in the evening

Now for the first time in two days I am hungry, a little
I have read *Journey to the East* to them.
Margaret is reading *Alice in Wonderland* to them.
My hands are cold, it is the dexedrine.
It is the need for food, it is cold at the theatre.
The long high windows are open, the wind blows in.
The people are good, but there is no magic in them
So I am a guru—I am not, as I was, among friends.
There has this change occurred.

8. She goes to sleep

Lies down, in the jewelled room.
The red light glimmers from the votive light on the altar
Shadow of Shiva dancing on the wall
"See how Christ's blood streams in the firmament":
surely this heaviness is not my own.
Premonition of some sorrow yet unborn
Tempest-tossed on the pillow, and going to sleep in the
    study
In my clothes
It is safer there, the inner sanctum
more easily defended
I shut my eyes
and watch the jewels that bounce against the lids
Entombed in this sepulchre, abandoned house
till the fingers of morning poke me awake again.

Weeks later, and it is grey, as it was grey. No change. The April drips onto everything. The clocks have been set ahead an hour, confusing me. We have got rid of the theatre, the press is humming. Alan is writing, book after book gets started. The springs that are behind me, our concerns. We were concerned about so many things. The war in Vietnam has started. World War III. Looming large in grocery stores, across the city. "God help my children," said the little Puerto Rican when I bought milk, "and God help your children / all we can do is pray." The gentle Buddhist on the radio, bowing and smiling, telling us it was "not good thing" that we did. I am making the repros of Huncke's book, and almost thru with A.B.'s. The rain has fallen on the colored clothes three days and nights. They hang limp & grey on the line, and wait for some sun.

How many things it was we used to care for! I read old notebooks with some amazement, dusting them off & typing, preparing to sell them. Alan is here, we shall not leave each other. He is writing a story about killing me. Jonas Mekas is renting our theatre. In my notebooks I come upon the four witches' Sabbaths, one of them falls on a Friday, end of this week.

Witches' Sabbaths:	February 2
Eve of May	April 30
Lammastide	August 2
All Hallow's Eve	October 31

This week went to Newark with Jimmy, and saw them all dance. Saw a dance that was made of mourning, the peices of it hung like tears in their hair and on their cheeks. I could have sworn they were weeping, was it sweat? Cut off at the ankles, because the stage was too high, they pinned black shawls over their golden schmattas.

Har, Har, Hou Hou
danse ici, danse la
joue ici, joue la

What are you brewing, stirring up there in your cauldron, in the leaden skies. Swung down like a lid on us. You, stirring with your unscorchable finger, stirring and tasting, the spittle falls occasionally on our heads. We wait. Leaning against the walls our anger makes. Crossing one foot over the other, and folding our arms. Where are the soft words of spring, the unreachable longings? The sighs, the endless turning over in bed? I sleep like a man exhausted, a laborer, dirty and leaden, and wake to no new love. Occasionally stirs in my dream like a memory, the taste of fleshly loving, it is enough. When I awake I desire no new union. Alan and I amble onward hand in hand, two besotted weary junkies filled with light. Union with Shiva, the most anyone can desire. But even the flowers are blooming badly, white hyacinth I bought grows brown at the tip, after only two days, and I water it enough. Sometimes I think that nothing will grow again, we will turn, a red planet under a lead grey sky, where the sun, indifferent, never penetrates.

It was thinking of you I bought the hyacinth. Hyacinthos. Which you loved, always, their phallic shape, their

127

Easter connotations. *Christos voskres.* The man in the honey store wrote it on his window. The women coming and going all week from church. Baskets with new linen on them, and it embroidered. The newly dyed eggs arranged to go visiting. Last month I wanted to plant them on your grave. The hyacinths. Ordering Alan's limousine (three days' folly) to take me to the Ossining cemetery. But the air was even colder then, nothing would grow, nothing would live in it. I thought of getting out of a black limousine, while the indomitable, taciturn driver waited for me. Getting out, all dressed, my high heels denting the soft ground, and walking to you, kneeling on that earth. How you would enjoy that, you enjoy so many things.

Like the sight of me in my shop these afternoons. The shop I cannot help feeling that you gave me. Golden yellow and red. Where I putter and print, it is warmer there than at home. Where the daylight fades slowly around me, the street comes alive. A.B.'s book is nearly finished. The pages stretch over the red velvet bench, and the folding chairs that I took from our emptying theatre.

It is May at last, it has grown warm at last. The sun, hot, beating down on my head, on the roofs of this house. Alex and Mini playing on the roof. Forty days till summer. About. I work on Eighth Avenue in the languid air. That stirs about the languid shapes of people. The people cruising, walking, calling to one another, in the soft spring twilights. Radio plays while I work, it plays show tunes mostly (boss hates "serious music"), tonight it played "Maria Elena," and

I was six years old, at a Brooklyn apartment, wind was blowing in from outside, thru some long French windows, Aunt Ella sat at a piano, playing "Maria Elena." It was Before the War, those spring twilights were also sombre. The time has come to put a stop to it, war and the memory of war, woven into our lives. For the past fifty years, at the least. I shall print a thousand Stop America Now signs, in red ink. I shall plaster them over Manahatta. This afternoon, in my study, Archie Shepp and I thrashing out the respective provinces of our races. I gave to him and his, the material world. ALL THE REFRIGERATORS THEY COULD USE. The kingdom and the power and the glory. Pray they will not settle for so little. And kept for us this corner: remembrance and rituals. The uses of the past. The turning seasons. Altars for prayers, the customs of the tribe, all the tales we will not forget, when all is forgotten. Kirby Doyle & I remembering them in the caves. Recounting them, in the slow spring twilights of later. What India kept alive for us for so long. Outside all night now sirens, they are rushing to the aid of the stricken monster. WE ARE THIS MINUTE KILLING CHILDREN IN SANTO DOMINGO. Their cries on this soft spring night. Floating over the trees. We are taking apart the jungles piece by piece in Asia. I feel Michael's anger, Philip's restlessness across America. The continent trembles with it. Allen's horror. Out there in his Prague cafes. What must we do? We must form a living chain, somehow, locking hands from your death to the songs we will sing in the evenings, around the fires. We must lock hands and stop them, somehow, with our flesh. I keep asking myself What Would Shelley Have Done? What would he do? What is he doing now? Archie knows, to educate, to bring to pass. For him it is still simple.

Every night now for three or four weeks they have been sawing in the later hours, after midnight, say, in the house just north of us. A deserted house, with pigeons in its windows. Over forty or fifty years old those pigeon nests. Thick, white, crusted with droppings, nests past all workmanship. The sound of their cooing wakes me in the morning. But in the night, the sound of sawing instead. I think of the armies of bums who might live inside. With electric saws. Trying not to call attention to themselves, sawing only at times when no one (almost) might hear them. I remember the bums that lived in the building next to ours on Amsterdam Avenue. Pulling a window board loose to get in at night. In spite of the rats and the garbage, living there.

What has spring become? My flesh has almost left me. There is no question now of sleeping with anyone. I remember the longing for George last year this time. One night or two when Louise was hearing Sonny Rollins and we were alone in the studies, each of us working. The magic spring wove about us and the ghosts of the house, George going out to the roof to play his flute. This year he came and sat a long time by my bed, I was sick, a little, we spoke of many things, most of them strange, the paths we were going, mine is so in and back, and then he kissed me goodnight, there were too many thousand years between us. Between last year and this. Whose I am now. How I possess myself. The love I seek. Thru the streets they are prowling, they are the human creatures. "Just like the cats" said Jeanne of

Joanne. I remember that world, it has refrigerators. I have made my last attempt to live in it. I wish it well. Last year at this time, Alan and I contemplated fleeing for a week or weekend to a motel, almost any motel, to be alone together and without Hermses who were continually making chaos. Nalota frightening Mini out of her mind, Nalota stealing jewels, beads, scarabs, boxes of food, and hiding all, all in her bed! We did not flee then, we stayed, we did *Guinevere* and *The Blossom*, it was perhaps our last chance to flee in the flesh.

Archie reminded me of so many things. Of so many books I read, long, long ago. When Lee Pagano had a sandal shop somewhere downstairs, somewhere on McDougal Street. With folksings in the evening. The boy Francesco from anarchist Spain, his father from Spain anyway, him with no papers and going to be deported, sent back there, where Franco would do whatever he does with such people. Francesco, whom Lee spoke of with such love, when imprisoned here, awaiting deportation, was asked to ply his usual trade (he was a baker) in the prison kitchen. Replied he, "I will do nothing to support this house." And sailed soon after, one or two cheerful letters, they had met him; and were taking him to see his mother somewhere in the hills. No other word, he is probably dead in a ditch.

THE STATE AND REVOLUTION by Lenin. THE STRATEGY OF WORLD REVOLUTION by Trotsky. THE SOUL OF MAN UNDER SOCIALISM, Oscar Wilde. WILLIAM MORRIS. "I WILL DO NOTHING TO SUPPORT THIS HOUSE." BAKUNIN. LEON KRAMER in his little anarchist store. His crippled wife, his sullen, stupid daughter. Grandpa in the park, preaching to the bums. About love, it was, we must all love one another. The park lights shining green through the leaves of trees. Those eternal benches, hedges, dog-shit, silence. The silence of city nights in the springtime. When the island once more becomes holy.

The spring that you and Alan left each other. I would drop Jeanne off at the school bus, Sheridan Square, and walk slowly back, I was heavy with Mini. Alan would meet me often, and go with me. We would stop at the Beefburger on Eighth Street, and eat wineburgers and chocolate malteds. A certain confusion of loyalty, for part of that time you were still living with me, and both of you so lost, really unhappy. Sometimes leaving Jeanne would meet Peter Hartman and we would go to the Bagel for breakfast together. Speaking of Jeanne or of Latin gerunds.

After you moved out of my house on Fourth Street that year you lived for some time on Avenue D on some forbidding sixth or seventh floor. I would call you often, and ask you to come to breakfast, one of my favorite ways always to see people. And you would reply that you didn't want to come out, you were work-ing on a circle. You would tell me the circle was going well, or going badly. You told me about one that had blue in it. One of them hangs still on my wall. You are totally in it.

On Monday took Mini to school, the walk to Avenue D monotonous, and then walked slowly back, stop-ping on Avenue C for a kerchief, a hood I finally found, so to go to church (decided on St. Bridget's, because of Frank, partly), and went to St. Bridget's, clutching in my hand new twenty-five-cent hood, royal purple, like my turban and thinking cap, and at the steps met DeeDee and Bobbie Driscoll, and bought them coffee, DeeDee lovely in an olive green dress and blue polo shirt, I admired her for it, she felt terrible, beat and tired, and had been fighting with Bobbie and they both have to get out of their place, which is the old Michael Smith place where Johnnie Dodd has made a wall of 160,000 George Washington stamps with the profiles cut out, and where they have been staying, but in spite of all she looked lovely with her dyed red hair, it is the west coast tradition and a kind of noblesse oblige, girls look lovely, even under the most adverse of circumstances. Bobbie looked beat, he will not live very long. Drug has him, DeeDee knows this. Bought them coffee, DeeDee had a roll as she called it, I explained to the lady that means a Danish on this coast. Bobbie tied up and turned on in the men's room. They went on their way to find Ondine, I went to the church and lit a candle for you, a seven day one, for which I did not pay. To Mary. The only one there I can trust at all, for I see the Kali in her whenever I look. The glass of the candle was blue. Blue and gold the light shone thru it.

I HAVE A FLUTE. A double flute, brown wood, from Yugoslavia. Given me by John Fles. I am learning to play it. It is not easy. The dreams have told me a flute, a piece of jade, and always to wear a sari. Perhaps one summer for each, but they will all come. These are the rules the dream told me:

To eat but once a day
To take no meat
To sleep no more than four hours a night
Except once a week, when I shall sleep six to eight
hours
To meditate every morning before I begin my
day's work
To write each day after I meditate
To study each day
To fast for three days before the new moon
And three days before the full moon
To recite the mantra 108 times daily
Perhaps one of those a year. Ten years for those.

Last month, on the day before Easter I cleaned my house. DeeDee helped me, the children were coming home from Grandma's, Alan was coming back from his father's farm. She said that she couldn't help but remember, that two years ago at this time, on Easter we had gathered at my house in Topanga Canyon. Do you remember? You danced with DeeDee while Kirby glowered in the doorway. Wally dancing with Shirley, George with Louise, all proper. The triple-jack we drank so much of. The phonograph playing the Crystals over and over. Billy Linich. Jim Elliott took our pictures out by the rock, looking like a bunch of delinquent minors who happened to have had children. The little house literally shook with the feet and the music. We ate well, too, god knows what it was we ate.

And remembering all this, DeeDee wanted to have another Easter feast. OK I said. But nothing came of it. She was to cook a roast that was in the freezer of the house where she was staying. Ed and Zen looked forward to it, they came for a feast, I gave them cold chicken and fruits. DeeDee never got here, and I did nothing about it. Margaret wanted to, I think, a lot. But my feast now I am finding is the equinox, that is perhaps when Dionysius rises. Also I kept Good Friday.

May 9. Last night I worked late, on Eighth Avenue and Twentieth Street. Large plate glass window looking out on that avenue, full of cruising whores, slow cruising police cars. A damp & chilly spring night. The FM radio playing all sorts of junk into the empty (except for me) room but I too lazy to get up & change it. Heard therefore among the rest "Black Bottom," a song which brought me to that May we came back to the city, two Mays ago only it was and the city was blooming, was blossoming, full of movies, plays, dances, and high excitement, every night there were two or three places to choose from, where to go, what to see, who to visit. John Wieners lived on East Fifth Street, on the top floor in a pad full of mad amphetamine junkies drawing pictures, in a dirty bed, always high, a little worn out. John Daley lived four doors down, on the top floor in a long pad full of people. DeeDee and Freddie lived there with him a while, and DeeDee presented to the place some fake leather draperies (black) which were much prized. Said draperies later moved on to Debbie Lee's when John Daley went to Rome. I last saw them hanging in Debbie's house on Eleventh Street, two days after Freddie killed himself, hanging there in the arch that divided the rooms. It is easier to give up passion than sentimentality I think, hearing Alan cough from his study. John Wieners had hepatitis that spring, we were living at the Broadway Central, Alan & I, and then we moved into Clive Matson's house, which was a top-floor apartment in one of those small inner buildings that they used to build in the courtyards between blocks. Clive stayed with Erin and we lived there for a week or two, debating and gathering strength for the getting of this house, where I pray to live & dwell for a good many years. After a while at Clive's Alan said the city was unbearable (he had his May disease as he does now)—and we went out to Greenwood Lake to stay at the empty cottage of my mother. We took John Wieners with us to help him recover from his hepatitis, he had been thrown out of the hospital for stealing spikes off the trays. John went to sleep in a little bedroom at the lake house and slept and ate for a week with only occasional forays to the bathroom or patio. It was about this time that "Black Bottom" entered the picture. Jimmy Waring was preparing an evening for the Pocket Theatre to be called the *Pocket Follies* and he asked Alan to do a piece for it. Alan consented, and asked Jimmy to direct him. Jimmy consented. Alan bought the music and the record. I remember endless sessions later in Brooklyn, with the phonograph, with Alan learning the words (he never could learn the words of anything) and shouting, singing, going on and on with that song. Jeanne loved it. The house rang with it. Silly place full of wallpaper. Alan more or less learned it. Jimmy never directed him in it, avoided the issue somehow, Alan with blind faith went on, sure that Jimmy would make it work at the last minute. Jimmy never did. Alan finally went on in a huge red cape and sang "It's my party and I'll cry if I want to, cry if I want to, cry if I want to, cry if I want to..." etc. up the aisle and out of the theatre. But last night, hearing that song, I remembered that Alan, working so hard to learn his song, filled with what energies and faith that Jimmy would do it somehow, working harder than I ever saw him work, except for when he learned the lines of *The Blossom*. That was an Alan I loved, and it is easier to get rid of passion than sentimentality.

I remember when Mini was born, it was about this time of the year, in Manhattan General Hospital, and there were two Chinese ladies in the ward with me, they had just had babies. There were eight of us in the ward, we all had a pitcher of ice water beside our beds of course, but the two Chinese ladies had each a pitcher of hot water, because, as the nurse told me, the Chinese like to drink hot water especially in the morning, and how beautiful that was, it epitomized New York to me, that concern that can happen here for the way each one does it. Now it is three years later, things have gone from bad to worse, we always knew they would, but we never quite believed it, and they have. From bad to worse. Cuba was bad enough, but now it is Santo Domingo and I feel a lot like the Germans must have felt, the ones who left and the ones who tried to stop it. Jean at the pottery shop is leaving for a place in the country, or else, as she said, a place out of the country. We will soon be driven out of our house, and where will we go then? Somewhere in North America we suppose, but we do not know. *Come and Be Killed* was the title of a mystery by Josephine Tey. It was not a book I ever read. But one night, dreaming, I dreamt that Josephine Tey was waiting for me by the catalogue of the Print Room in the library on Forty-Second Street where I had been planning to spend the day. I had never read anything by Josephine Tey, but I knew that she wrote mysteries. I went next door to Zella's house, and asked her if she had any Josephine Tey I could borrow and she gave me a book. Its title was COME AND BE KILLED. I didn't go to the library that day. It is like that now. But where can we go? I am asking this thing of you who will survive it, and you who will come after. Where could we have gone? I want to go to Ed Sanders at the Peace Eye Bookstore and say Ed, we are all the smartest and the strongest people in the country, what aren't we doing that we should be doing? How can we stop it? Stop America Now. He will not know, but perhaps we will think of something. Is there a war on? There is a war on. It will be called the Third World War. Or perhaps the last phase of the Period of World War. Alan will survive it, because he wants to. So will Herbert Huncke. Strong, bright and ruthless people will survive it. I do not want to see what will come after. I will survive it if my children do, to simply care for them. The simplicity and horror of these things. I read Miss Stein, writing in France in the thirties, and she says, perhaps the war will not come. She is quite sensible and brave about it. I am an Italian woman and I have no need to be either sensible or brave. I am neither. Dispassionately, from a distance, I can look at my life, saying yes, the first of the inevitable things was the abortion, then leaving Roi, her marriage. The first place with no turning back, the death of Freddie. Next, these lives run a pattern always, she will go into exile. Into some foreign country, continue her work there. Alan looks ahead, seeing a book a month from the press. What I see is simply the next four books, and then? Wherever my life takes me, I will go. I WILL NOT BUDGE TILL THEN. This perturbation. Part of the Dance. So be it.

On Second Avenue they walk, the people. Who make New York so dear. They are lumpy & dumpy, they are Howie Kanowitz, who is always happy, and Helen De Mott, who is stooped and funny-eyed. With a look humble, with a spirit indomitable. They are not intimates, but they are friends. There are no more intimates, as Miss Stein might say, we have entered a period of high civilization. There are no electric lights in our house anymore. We do not raise our voices after nightfall. Peace falls on us, out of the sky, as the dark of the moon approaches we grow dim. The spirits, says Alan, speak to him from the walls. Come out and play with him in the darkened rooms. Jeanne sleeps with two candles on a chair beside her. Not liking the dark as we do. I type in my shop, on an old grey machine. It is called poverty, a form of riches.

It is hot, like summer, with thunderstorms and certain downpours, and yet it is only May. I have just been to Debbie Lee's new house on Great Jones Street with Jeanne, who was to take dance class. I thought, I will go up and visit Debbie Lee, there has been no visiting of that sort since Freddie died, and it really isn't right, I thought, not to visit just because there's no Freddie, why it used to be that on a spring Sunday morning I would go up to their house on East Eleventh Street for bread and coffee and amphetamine and all that glee and hospitality. For a while, when there was no hot water heater in our house (every spring the hot water heater goes, or the ice box, or the electricity, every spring the people who collect bills become rampant, it is something one gets accustomed to after a while, just that time of year, they do it in the fall too, but not so badly because they are all so disorganized from their summer vacations, but in the spring they do it well, all those people, they have had all winter from the time the holidays are over on till the warm weather to prepare, and so spring is a time of summonses, of eviction notices, of heaters and stoves and refrigerators and washing machines breaking down) and last year there was no hot water and I would go in the morning, of a Sunday, escaping the house full of kids and full of Hermses and Herms smells, and take a bath in Freddie and Debbie's house in the center of their kitchen. Bringing bubble bath which sometimes I'd leave them as a present. I was thinking of all these things when I went up the stairs at Great Jones Street, thinking Debbie Lee would be pleased that I had come for a visit, but lo and behold, her door was open, yes, but she wasn't there, don't know where she was, but now thinking it over I think maybe she's at the Bridge Theatre, because they are rehearsing *The Sideshow*, which was the play Alan threw out of the East End Theatre by shaking Jimmy Waring. So I left Jeanne there in case Debbie got back, left her in Al Hansen's place and came here to the shop to type, can't type at the house because the electricity is off, we live by candlelight, it is a thing one gets accustomed to. In the nights I come home from work and there is a candle burning in the hall on the high platform in front of what used to be Minerva's shield in *Love's Labor*. Glowing like a sun. And on up the crooked stairs, Alan lies in his study in all that candlelight, reading or writing a little on his machine. Our voices are soft, we navigate precariously in the semi-dark, searching out cans of tuna fish, jars of peanut butter. Or we lie in the bedroom reading, two candles by each of our heads. My proposed article on "Electricity and the Divorce Rate." How it is impossible to raise one's voice by candlelight, to fight and scream and throw things unthinkable. The dark would throw them back, as simply as that. And people are more beautiful and houses more clean, you can't see into the corners. One is slowed down. Our house is very pleased. The fridge stands open and idle, a dead machine. My big red typewriter waits to be used again. It is having a rest. In my study I sit at my desk with two candies on it, and answer my mail by hand—letters are flowing all around the country, as they haven't in months, one has so much more time in the dark.

June. The spring turns into summer, the year of our separation draws to its end, its last phase, your brother Kirby is in jail, I am learning a bit how to pray, how to meditate, there is so much to tell you. Footsteps of Mini & Alex on the stairs, the echo of bombs in the air, we are bombing Laos, are bombing Vietnam, are bombing Santo Domingo. We are spreading all kinds of rumors: that Mao is dead, that Chou En Lai is a devil, that we have been sent by God to save the world. By killing it, by poisoning the air, the water, the wheat, defoliating the jungles, perhaps we speak nothing but the truth. Perhaps we have indeed been sent by God. Perhaps we are saving the world, by turning its face back to the Mystery, away from the blackcloud science, back to the only knowledge that can save it now. The redemption of the earth thru blood and tears. Thru alchemy. Last year at this time the Hermses had moved in with Kirby, I visited you on Eleventh Street and you teased me for my certainty that George must stay here for his own salvation. George didn't stay, his salvation, and Kirby's, and ultimately yours and mine were all bound into this fact. The black theatre echoed the lines of *The Blossom*. You were in *Home Movies*, night after night. This year I have walked these mornings thru East Side streets, pushing Mini Jones in her stroller to nursery school, watching the fruit stands blossom, the markets, in the heat of the days. One morning, on First Avenue, it was 90 degrees and not yet 10 o'clock, glancing at a fruit stand I saw a small dark head that I thought belonged to Roi and my heart skipped a beat, did a funny thing that it hadn't done for years, it wasn't Roi and I walked on wondering why that particular sight had moved me so, I mulled it over as I pushed the stroller. And it seemed to me that I WAS IN LOVE WITH OBSCURITY. An unknown Roi, shopping for peaches on Avenue A, bowed a little by the weight of poems at home, the obscurity that echoes in *La Boheme*, that we are not accorded here in America, tho we are not accorded honor or peace either, they have pierced our darkness too, we don't have that. An unknown Roi, shopping for apples and berries to bring home to his family, poor and obscure, planning to go home, to write and study thru the day, to go out at night among other unknown poets drinking and talking the night long, a kind of youth we surely had a right to. NOT TO BE IN THE SPOTLIGHT. And I vowed then, futilely, vowed and prayed that darkness cling to me the days of my life. That I earn my bread and, my children's by the work of my hands, that the poems inside my head and in the air remain unnoticed, a puzzlement to humans.

Even then I knew "not this time," but I prayed. Came home, and horrified Alan with these thoughts. Like Blake, to turn the wheel of my printing press, unheeded and unheeding, not to speak on BAI or read at the Metro. To work and print and pray till the earth goes dry.

Allen Ginsberg crowned King of the May and thrown out of Prague, dwelling in England in all kinds of confusion. The war beginning, Alexander walking, Philip Whalen wanting to win a secret prize for poetry. I remember a spring I lay at Greenwood Lake. Crying my eyes out for Roi & for our baby. The one I was going to abort, I knew it, soon. And now Roi is leaving Hettie and moving to Harlem, to his repertory theatre, and Mini with braids goes down to play in the street, being fully old enough for that.

When do we read and when do we write, those are two of the things I have been wondering about, for instance, I have read thousands of books, yes, thousands of books, and I have never caught myself reading, or very seldom, very seldom caught myself at it, in the process of reading or of writing. True once in a while I look up from a book, and I find myself in a not-place, a different place than I while in the book thought I was in, perhaps I had been in Trollope country and I look up and find me, a lady in slacks of the twentieth century, true I have braids and my house smacks of earlier times, but it cannot be denied I am in slacks and overhead is an electric light which will sometimes go on if I decide to use it, I am not a Trollope lady at all. Or a Henry James. And so, in a backhanded way I have caught myself reading. The only other person I ever catch reading is Alan, yet nearly everyone I know has read thousands of books. It is as if they do it by osmosis. I became aware of this because I was talking to Herbert Huncke tonight about science fiction, and then when I came back from work the house being empty, Alan being off somewhere with Huncke, shooting horse, or seeing Bill Burroughs, and I being a little lonely in the still candlelit house, I went into the study and turned on the electric light there for the first time since the electric lights have been made to work again and when the room became flooded with that frenetic and strange glow I thought "this is light I could work in at night, it would keep me awake to work" and then not working went to the bookcase to find something to read, having dispensed with a finished Henry Miller and there began to look for *Childhood's End* or some of the Theodore Sturgeon Huncke had mentioned and then it occurred to me "When does Huncke read?" I had never caught him reading. I daresay no one has ever caught him reading, no one of my acquaintance. Perhaps there are days at people's houses when he curls up with a book and reads it from cover to cover. Or perhaps he says, in that polite way of his, "May I borrow this?" and walks off to the park, or his hotel room when he has one, with something and reads it. I wonder. It is such a mystery. For instance, I opened a book of Freddie's, a book by Stein which he had given me when he gave me all his books in 1962, that spring that Mini was born, that Alan went away. That Freddie left Houston Street and I lived a little sick and very scared on East Fourth Street. *Portraits and Prayers*. It is a very nice book, and I began to read here and there in it, some of the pieces I had heard Stein read on records, and I could hear her again, saying the lines, and so I indulged in that, and I thought about Freddie teaching Alan to read Stein, "read it out loud" he told him when he couldn't understand it, and Alan did, and then I wondered when Freddie had read Stein, this particular volume particularly. I know that he read when he lived in Westchester growing up, that Lorene Pruette taught him a good bit about reading, and I wondered if she taught him about Stein, or how he found that, I know that he found it before I did, for instance, he found it before I met him. I was still into the reading of *Portraits and Prayers*, I have never picked it up and just read it and I may be wrong but I have the feeling that Freddie did. Pick it up and just read it. Start and finish. There was something about the feel of that particular volume in my hands that told me somebody had done just that. We read in secret mostly. In the john, on the bus or train that takes us to school or to work, on the way to sleep. It is almost a forbidden activity, like shitting and screwing. It is as pleasurable which leads me to believe it shall be equally taboo in no time. I used to see O'Meara read the way I see Alan do it. Stretched out on a couch, blatantly. Not most people. Freddie reading Stein, Huncke reading Bradbury, John McDowell reading John Dickson Carr, Jimmy Waring reading *The Banquet Years*, Debbie Lee reading *The Secret of the Golden Flower*, me reading *The White Company*. I know I did because it is on a list of books I read in 1956, when I kept a journal and wrote down every day who I was screwing, who I was eating with, what I was reading, what I was writing, what I was studying. It made me feel the days weren't

145

utterly wasted. *The White Company* by Conan Doyle. Can't remember a word of it, but I remember the volume, a fat one, of the collected writings of Doyle, with two columns of type.

I have lots of time to wonder about things like this now where I work, perched one flight up above Eighth Avnenue, WPAT pouring its muzak at me all day, all night, the click of my typewriter scarcely an interruption, the pleasure of working with my hands at a "light box" thinking little thoughts about anything at all. The trips home across the city always different, an infinite number of ways to get there. Walks, taxis, buses, subways, on which I read. On the walks I think. Sometimes I read on the walks, but I usually think, remembering this or that. Today, in the afternoon, bright unbelievable sun, took a wrong turn off Seventh Avenue and found myself on Charles Street face to face with a yellow stucco building in which I'd nearly taken an apartment with Lori, a small lovely top floor, one large room, skylighted, and a tiny bedroom. Dazzlingly white, and for those days, terribly expensive, $100 a month. The lovely, clean white and blackness, the light there, and then tonight on Greenwich Street, walking home past the crowds of young men with henna'd heads who at 3 a.m. have still not found a lay, or in some cases are back again looking for more, I saw a store that advertised. "four captain's chairs" and remembered them on one of Lori's beautifully written, nervous, meticulous lists, "captain's chairs" in her inimitable hand. I thought again of how earnestly and terribly she had wanted the life she had outlined, so that she lent a kind of glory to it, and yet, really, how shabby and mediocre it was when you stepped out of the halo of her longing. I thought (turning on Eighth Street and waiting a little for a bus) that if desire, strong desire, were enough to make a thing happen, Lori would have had her white apartment, her "two-ply strathmore board," her harpsichords and captain's chairs. For the first time seeing perhaps it takes more than desperate hunger to bring something about. It takes some sanity. That the thing itself be not-mad. I don't know. It is soft early June, there had been violence in the city for some weeks, tonight is quiet, gentle except for the trucks. Mini has had her third birthday, with beads and clay and blocks and cakes and all. The children in gowns gathered again in front of the fire. Simply and naturally, as if this was their birthright. They played at cooking, with clay, which they pressed out on stones. No question in their heads where this house would be tomorrow. A mellow wisdom in their antics. I pause between typings and listen for Alan's steps. He does not come home, the house is very still. Vague hungers stirring. I shall go now to bed, say my mantra, sleep, tomorrow run errands, post office first, and the cleaners. Then work on the Genet book, typeset the English. Then go to work, meet Alan at the movies. Perhaps. The world stretches simply before me. A.B. has stopped waiting for his book, because it is out. Now Huncke waits for his book. I must get it out. Then Phil will be waiting behind him. Work for these hands. A pleasure. I must sleep.

Eileen Pasloff in Frank O'Hara's *Loves Labour* (by Will Mott)

Frankie Francine in *Loves Labour* (by Will Mott)

Alan Marlowe (by Daniel Entin)

Jimmy Waring and Deborah Lee in Waring's *Dances before the Wall*

Valda Setterfield and Alan Marlowe in *Murder Cake* (by Diane di Prima)

James Waring in *Self-Designed Costume* (by Daniel Entin)

Diane (by Daniel Entin)

summer

To exorcise the evil in the cold June air. The cold June air. Black with rainclouds and dust, swirls of death-mist hanging over the city. Strange mulatto creature with a hairy classical face, a bum or god? or a thief in the night, walking in circles on the sidewalk near my house, pink striped shopping bag under one arm, brown bag in one hand, all his possessions? He got to the corner, near the "HOTEL Hotel" and stood waiting. An hour later he was still there still standing waiting. I was coming back from a bookstore on Tenth Street. A line of seeming midgets, a long school-line of retarded children from the school on Fourth Street came up the block hand in hand led by a sickly woman teacher. They stopped at the corner till she told them to cross. They sent him reeling, him and his paper bags. I went inside the house and shut the door. Feeling even here the protections were weak. Due to imperfect performance of winter rites. No new mandala drawn on the door. I went upstairs, smelling death everywhere. Took Alex off the kitchen table, where he sat, chewing candles. Came to this shop, my last stand, green, yellow & red, pictures of Freddie & Frank on the walls. Where I was endlessly ill.

The incomprehensible evils of the weather. Almost no pigeons left on the city steps. A knot of subtle rhinestones on my desk. THE ARMY CARRIES CORPSES IN ITS WAGON. Is what the book warned. True enough. Let go.

Farewell to the dust-strewn brick and crumbling mortar. The crumbling structure of our lives together. Color of candlelight on all our flesh. Laughter of children wrapped in our wrapping round. Silence of high wood

157

beams, blue skylight light. Pictures like fire lighting up the rooms. Intricate twisted threads and wax and glass. A world where we stood or sat or lay with equal ease. The regal splendor of my purple couch. Quiet encroachment of that Tibetan god. Welcome encroachment, watch the world come down. A roman candle, my husband, spins away, sputtering, trying to think what he ought to say. Farewell to the red door that locked without warning, four times locking us in. The hearth, the heart of the house, where we roasted yams and pumpkins for the harvest. And burned a white birch log for the winter sun. Wide board, wooden floors aslant, wind thru the windows. Candle flames bending under that constant wind. High airy black space of the downstairs hall. The leaning staircase. Round table under round and yellow lamp-shade. Where we all met this time round, greeting each other. The mysteries of communion at that table. The jewelled gleam of brick wall from my study. The roof I sat on in the early mornings, playing my flute for the sun, and it warmed my bones. A fair exchange. Farewell to enormous bookcase, golden walls, to Alan's hash pipe standing filled on the table. While people peeped in from the hotel next door. The plants we grew on the roof, the *Blossom* painting. So hard to make a life, and hard to uproot it. An endless technical exercise.

July 3. It is hard to write here, it is a world (a shop) given over to other people. The serving of them. Herbert Huncke's story sits on the light table, waiting correction. David Henderson's manuscript sits on the mimeo table, waiting to be read. Outside the Fourth of July air lingers around us. Oppressive and heavy it sits down on my head. In the study one was fortified as in a tower. Safe from attack, ensconced at the head of the stairs. Here the opening of the door is always imminent, Timothy wanting to type, Don come to collate. I long to return this book to my cell to work on in silence. But shall not this summer, before this summer is over.

That is the nature of summer, has always been the nature of my summers. Vagrancy, confusion, a lightness of head. A clearness of vision, hands too weak to follow up on. The children gone off like planets or wandering stars. To sit in another constellation for a while. If I were younger I'd go to a beach and sleep. The old abandoned quarries up in Maine. The furnished rooms on Charles Street, the park at dawn. The trips to Provincetown, to Beacon, to Kennebunkport. Some of my colleagues still roam in that kind of sun. John Wieners at Spoleto. The conclave at Berkeley. I sit in the cool space and reaches of this shop. Press protected with white oilcloth from the dust. Walls clean, painted bright yellow. The damp and shade of being downstairs from the street.

Of course I am haunted by the roofs of summer. Of last summer in particular. The watchers that crept behind you on the roof at Ridge Street. The sun that streamed in those windows, incredible view. As if it were Baghdad and we were in a tower. Sun on those roofs the light and hint of the river. The mattresses I lay on with you and Kirby. In the golden dawn, in a world shining inside a crystal. The crystals of A that you shook out on my palm. The whispers of shreds of satin, fallen to tatters. The comings and goings of that mysterious tribe. It was not last summer, a thousand years ago. We divided the

Beck estate, each finding a schmatta, a jewel, a picture to their taste. The following season divided your estate. The tribe will meet again in another aeon. Moving closer each time to light, and total recall.

There are summer birds, and children on the street. Just at my shoulder height, a few feet away. July is a menace always, when I think of July I think of the walk I took thru Tompkins Square Park with Peter Hartman. It was Fourth of July weekend the hoods sat in the trees with firecrackers and threw them down around us. How angry I was with Peter for that he walked faster and faster. No calm, no animal instinct to preserve him. I think of the trips to Bayside when I was a child. Only a little older than Jeanne is now. Trips to Aunt Evelyn's house where I was a person. Was treated like a person, allowed to read. To talk about what I was thinking. The park near Aunt Evelyn's where I lay on the grass. Looking up thru the dark green leaves at the too blue sky. Some kind of menace in the heat of it. The blue sky and the blinding sun, that peace. As I lay on my back and felt the earth move under me. Felt its breath and its pulse and the arching of flesh as it turned.

As I lay on my back years later in Jersey hayfields. While Clody and Lori made mad love not far away. Grasshoppers leaped on my breasts and leaped off again. I looked at the sky thru the yellow and brown of the hay. Ground lumpier than the ground had been in that park and this time it was August. The earth still breathed.

We pursued their pleasure thru the green grass of various estates. With squareset ponds lined on both sides with plaster statues. Twenties imitations of the Greek. And driveways, entrances columned and silent. Beside lakes and ponds we would pause and capture pleasure. And swim or drown, stepping off a rock into a whirlpool. Clody's red-gold hair, large beautifully formed thighs. How unfitted we all were for living at all. No guile in us, no malice. The sun beating on that water roused up mosquitoes. We sauntered back dripping to the hot broken car and found our way back to Clody's wooden house.

The dusty smell of old hot cars in summer. Or of bus terminals in Flushing where you catch the bus to Bayside. Of the store Uncle Artie stopped in (I was younger then) on my way to his house with him and bought me a toy. What it was I don't remember, but I remember the mysterious high reaches of wooden shelves packed with old faded colored boxes with toys inside. I remember too a smell of tobacco and a kind of shade, the shade of a place where the sun never hits directly. As it never hits this shop where I sit typing. Large square maroon chairs they had at Aunt Evelyn's house, raised ruggy nap on the upholstery. White bookcase, with books too hard for me to read. *Penguin Island, Moby Dick*, a console radio. That stood on the floor in one corner of the apartment just as a television would stand now. And there I would sit in the mornings in the sunlight when I was seven (this was before Bayside) and listen to one soap opera after another, while Aunt Evelyn scrubbed the kitchen floor till it shone. A low table covered with glass with some picture under it that I almost remember. A picture Artie would tell me stories about. I would play some kind of game, which consisted of getting thru a gate built by Artie's arm as he lay on the square couch with his hand on the table. That the glass on that low white table finally cracked is something I remember only dimly.

It is hard to write of the summer in the summer. All other seasons lead to it, all thoughts of other seasons move imperceptibly back to what we did in a summer, but with the warm air pressing down on us and the sounds of kids out of school climbing the stoops, jumping on the cars, the dust in the areaways, the cats languid, the flies coming in to see what the garbage is like, it becomes impossible to think or write of summer as an objective fact. The things we did last summer. Alan went two days ago to the Houston Street pool. The showers are turned off, there is no water, even I am careful and turn off the faucets tightly, no longer angry at the world and thinking "the sooner they run out the better" but remembering and finally learning from Ohsawa's tirade against the waste of a grain of rice. If everyone in the world he wrote wastes one grain of rice a day two billion grains of rice are wasted and many could eat who are now starving. This is no longer the "land of plenty" they wrote about in those long flat geography books (book which I used to pile all my other books on in two even piles. Books which changed the color of their covers every year, I do not remember their content at all except that New York was the Empire State, the best state, and this was the best country, a land of plenty.) In which they are draining the lakes to get water for cities. In which there are no clear streams. In which California and Arizona fight over the Colorado River. And the buffalo run off cliffs, killed by the thousands, the stink of that meat festering in the sun rose with no good odor to the nostrils of the Great Spirit. Of that we may be sure. (A large fly is trying to get in my mu tea.) But it was a mistake at this point to go to the Houston Street pool where you wanted last year to make your water ballet / where you used to swim every day, taking Jeanne sometimes with you. The things we did last summer. Walking up from Ridge near Grand and to the pool. Or home, if you were me to change your clothes. Fire signs have trouble always swimming. Tho Alex has learned at last to like his bath. They are shooting off firecrackers in the streets. The fly has decided to try to leave the store.

July 6. I came down the stairs in our dark house—no lights, gas, candles everywhere and a hibachi to cook on. But the candles mostly out except where I was reading and where Alan sat typing, mostly out to save them, to cut down their cost from what it had been—$1.50 a day—to something reasonable, something we could manage. Came down, avoiding the bag of coal that sits at the head of the second flight of stairs always since I moved it out of my study but couldn't get it down the stairs and creaked on down to the first landing. Paused at the window and looked for a glimpse of the moon. Nothing doing. No moon. On down the next flight, which is lit by the reflection of the orange lights they set in the traffic island in the middle of our street, so that people won't run into it or into each other. People do anyway, every night. Often the orange lights are smashed and dark and the island is strewn with diamonds of broken glass. Tonight they have just put up a new yellow sign with nine red dots on it in three rows of three each and new lights in the light-thing, and they are on, blinking, first the east & west ones, then the north & south. On and off. Endlessly. When the east and west ones go on there is a spear of orange light (the eastern light only) which juts up the pole and into the window. Bouncing in the hall. The north and south make a wider softer light. Blink. Blink. I walked into the kitchen and blew those two candles out too. Jeanne's was on and there is one, in the bathroom. Should be enough. Blew these out close together, one right after the other, not watching the smoke of the first by the light of the second as I had done upstairs in the bedroom, the smoke there making shadows on the wall. This time, one two. And watched instead the two red ember-like wicks glowing in the dark of the kitchen. Picked up bag, down the other stairs. On the door to the street a light is glancing and flickering. Almost blink, blink. Almost that rhythm. It is the candle at the head of the stairs. Which has picked up from the street the rhythm of the orange light…

So many summer evenings like this I remember. Soft, langorous, stretching softly before me with the promise of a book, a peach, a walk. Soft sounds from outside. Alan says this year our life is harder than usual. I am not aware of it. I remember lying pregnant on the bed in Jeanne's room, a room all bare except bed, while Alan pulled up nails and tore at floorboards, anger in him always making me weep. When we made the house we now prepare to leave. Not at all sure we should be leaving it. In that no other thing presents itself. No house / says come and take me.

The Ukrainian band was warming up a little tonight as I walked up the street from the shop. Almost it started to play those eternal songs it had played summer after summer, the year we moved in they played and I painted the inside of the long cupboard. Stained the large new bookcases brown, my large stomach getting in the way. Alan worked fiendishly straightening everything out. The baby came in August, I was tired. And sad most of the time, from the effort of keeping Alan from being sad.

Different that summer tho. The glow of our return to New York. How have I failed him, the husband, strange that I should come to this, write about it. It is karma, I suppose, I feel it as such, as a point where we have met, baffled, many times. Habits ingrained for thousands of years in both of us, holding us from the conclusions we must reach. I think of various ways to break out of it. All of them unreal, like taking a hotel room for three or four nights, not letting him know where I am, see what changes by then. All childish as hell, unlikely they will work. And meanwhile, work on the books in the yellow shop. Cry more than usual, even for me. Know I should study and write, fill my days and nights. "As the sun at midday," a glow to the roots of my hair.

Yes we were pleased to return, to come back to it. Now we are older, more cautious, don't plan to go far—Brooklyn or Hoboken the limits we conceive. In the shop next door to mine they have put on a blues record, Lightnin' Hopkins, and someone is coughing. They are walking around. This is new. There has been no summer like this. When I type in a yellow shop, and Alan prints. I see us in no Brooklyn, rain or shine.

July 7. In all my dreams this week it has been winter. Last night you came to my house with Kirby Doyle and we ate sardine sandwiches on rye bread with onions, ravenously. You asked Alan for his blue wool shirt to keep you warm, trying on dresses and shirts indiscriminately. I embraced John Wieners in the long dark alleys of another city. Rich dreams, full of rain, full of those I love. Sports cars full of baseball players whizzing past. A bus that took me home, delivered me in New York so that I could get up.

Alan searches ravenously for a house. With foreknowledge Splitting Apart, I do nothing at all. Jeanne jumps rope outside, the pavement sounds of feet and rope, the garbled rhythm of her jingle. It is cool this summer, there have been few nights of crowded streets and stoops, crowded doorways with people playing guitars and radios. A chaste and chastened season.

And so it goes this shop is our anchor, the work in this shop our hope. The children are scattered, quite against our will. A fever to be free is laid on me. A wish to stand clear of any embroiling involvements. No husbands, lovers, roommates, no other grown-ups horning in on my scene. Alone with my children to be printing books. I wait and see if a house shows that will house us. All together. If it does not, will we separate easily. If we do, I shall be triumphant and guilty, not knowing whether I merely had foreknowledge, or if my malicious will brought this about.

July 8. It is midafternoon, we have just returned from Brooklyn where we were looking at houses on tree-lined streets. Next door in the shop a man is rattling about, slamming things recklessly and angrily. I imagine that he has found something similar to what I found in my bathroom when I got here this afternoon—the sink had somehow backed up and there were waterfalls and floods of water falling on the bathroom floor. Luckily the floor is full of holes—hardly a floor at all and most of the water fell right on thru to the cellar without flooding anything in the shop. I did go tell the superintendent about it but he wasn't there, only a sweet old white-haired Polish woman whom I didn't want to disturb and so explaining as best I could I backed my way down again and back to the shop. Hearing the man next door slam around his place, I think about how long it has taken me not to be angry whenever a typical slum calamity occurs. It's almost as if New York teaches you to be angry—at stopped-up toilets, at roaches and fallen ceilings, backed-up gurgling sinks. Is it because you KNOW the landlord owes it to you that all these things work properly (as if a clogged drain were not, indeed, an act of God). It was in California where the cesspool backed up incessantly, where the fireplace smoked and the water supply precariously depended on our paying the water bill, that I learned that anger has no place in these things. (The calm of George and Louise with no plumbing at all, shitting in the woods.) So that finally one winter day in New York, our first year in this house, I awoke to the rain and tired from having recently had Alex and found the kitchen floor totally flooded, water dripping from innumerable holes in the ceiling under some of which Alan had thoughtfully placed our pots before he had gone to bed. Hardly a way to get between the drips to the bathroom, much less to the kitchen sink, and Jeanne late for school, the pots overflowing. Sent her back to bed to sleep and I did the same after turning on the gas heater to dry the air a bit. And awoke several hours later to a glorious clear fall day, the floor quite dry from the heater, the pots capable of being emptied without much discomfort and Jeanne greatly cheered by the lack of school. So that confronted by the sink overflowing and no super in sight, I sat down on a very hard chair which I contrived to make a little more comfortable by piling on it the black velvet drapes I have for the other windows and read a little pamphlet by John Fles, which has been sitting here unread for many a day... while I listened to the trompings and angers that came thru the wall. Even sketched out a new book. Brooklyn has grown lovelier and I am pleased about it, though the house we saw today was too small for us.

July 12, 1965. And so it turns out that this summer is cooler than most, a blessing for Alan who fears and hates the heat, tho the people are shouting as much as if it was hot, they stand on their stoops arguing about the garbage in the hallways, they stand outside bars waiting to get in, or they smash the windows. Waiting for the heat which will propel them. On to some madness. The moon will be full tomorrow. Last night the moonstruck girls, cursing and charming, as I rode across Fourteenth Street on a bus, as I walked down Third Avenue to our erstwhile house. It is harder in this cool summer to remember summers past, the langorous slow heat, the bottles of iced white wine at the head of large beds, white sheets tumbled and full of sweat and come, the slender bodies of maidens from Washington Heights, the full-hipped bodies of maidens from New Canaan, the wondrous scents and turnings of the earth. How two small windows looked down on a dingy street, 521 East Fifth Street, which was home. How I worked that summer through, eating lunch on the docks, Front Street, watching the scum and green moss and old Trojans floating on the water. Peanut butter sandwiches on Pepperidge Farm bread. And a tomato. Involved in the saving of money which I gave Lori. The days which passed graciously under the summer sun. The smell of the tarred posts of the piers, the green moss on them. Lazy slapping of backwater never changed. Reading, the studying of Latin, in the lunchroom there. The coffee breaks full of poems, or answering letters. Powdered coffee, powdered milk, and powdered sugar. In a cup together, add hot water & read a lot while drinking. A loud pushy midget named Ray, with flashing rings. Who worked as a salesman, spent his weekends in the "Village"—to him a lewd suggestive sound to that.

The summer after I had a series of rooms, slept in Washington Square, lived a long time with a long, dull boy who had a room on Waverly Place. A boy so long his feet stuck out of his room. Almost. They did when he slept on the floor, which he sometimes did, for there were times when as many as four of us slept in that tiny room. The bed, the floor, the chair, all covered with bodies. No window, only a skylight which opened, or on cooler days had a drape drawn across it. This long-armed boy would stand in the center of that little room and be able to reach everything in it without moving, reaching from high shelf for book to low table with hot plate, making tea, changing stations on the radio. A good sweet boy who was good and dear to me. In the fall I left him for freedom, and out of boredom.

The summer after that was a series of trips, mostly hitchhiking thru the reaches of the dingy north. The Berkshires to Tanglewood, to Jacob's Pillow, full of mosquitoes, sleeping out on the paths in the woods with Joan O'Meara or in a pine grove, Bobi Schwartz among trees, a faun in a distorting mirror. What was it? His smile? The rehearsals at Tanglewood free, the wideness of the hills there, the small white towns with church and post office just picture postcards to us, places we passed thru, no sense then of the dreariness of their lives, the stifling smells of the houses. A strange mountain town I stopped at once with Ray when he came hitching with me, stopping to see someone who turned out not to be home. Hiking to the town, asking at the post office where the house was (take the road thru the woods till you pass a potato barn and then turn left). Trying to find out what was a potato barn. Finding it. Going on. To the strange, still clearing, with insects at play in the hot sun, the house on its hinges locked and silent. Resting there a while, and finding a way in. The Indian rugs, the books, the people returning. The boy we went to see gave me a Welsh grammar. Our return downhill to the road, the lack of rides. Trucks going by in the silence. The ride we finally got back down the Taconic. Dawn over the Hudson valley seen from the side of the road where the driver had pulled over to go to sleep. How we lived a lot on a special kind of ice cream soda made with ginger ale and vanilla ice cream—good pep drink and killed hunger.

The house we found in the Berkshires, silent Dutch man who drove us there, a pilot he said, with an apartment in Riverdale where we spent the night. No come on really, just the two of us O'Meara and I curled up to sleep in one of his beds. At dawn setting off for Monterey, Mass., a huge friendly New England house. A fireplace stretching the full length of one room, a table that twenty could eat at easily. The plenty of German countries when they are prosperous. Butter in tubs, yellow-haired boys still toddling, two or three women. The windows white-curtained, New England, the four-poster beds. A lake for to swim and fish.

Reminding much of the other lake further back. Closer to my childhood, at the far end of my childhood. Though that one was more open, more under the sky, the lake the Ruthels had was hidden by trees, a clearing at the end of a path thru the woods, reminding one somewhat of the dream sequence in *Les Enfants Terribles*. The other lake I remember belonged to Boo. At Wheaton Farm, Audre and I spoke of it again this morning. Wheaton Farm, huge horse barns, but no horses by then, a house that had been an inn at the time of the revolution. Spinning wheels still there, huge rooms, a classic simplicity not to be found at Monterey. First trip there as a school girl still in college, still frightened slightly of Boo's father, of whom one had heard terrifying things, was lovely, there were herons on the lake, I have perhaps somewhere still a picture of those days: Lori and Eri and O'M and Gloria and me standing in the sun with Helmie, Boo's brother. Second trip with O'M and Brandy, new dyky friend of ours, looking and acting like any other young hood, who drove us in an old car thru a hundred and fifty miles of the wrong direction (she took a wrong turn out of Hartford in the dead of night). We finally arrived, there was no Boo's family. An old black caretaker and his family who fed us outside on the lawn in a glorious red sunset, we moved out the phonograph and played the B minor mass as the sun set over the lake, behind the herons, red and pink, the sky orange, streaked purple, and cool air, flat fields for once seeming peaceful and good, not claustrophobic. And revealed to us then, as from time to time in glimpses as though a veil is suddenly swept aside, the easeful and good life, gracious, that that house was built for, a life this century has turned its back on, the good we seek is no longer of the senses, but the peace and order of that visit remains, another manner of being on the earth.

Another summer we went to another house of Boo's, this one on the Massachusetts shore, not a happy shore that shore, the Cape cuts it off from the open sea, there are no real waves, no "surf" as Lori complained. We took the "milk train from New York," there were many of us. And Lori fell in love with Joan O'Meara. Sat up all night on that train full of sailors on leave (it was still the Korean War) and arrived sometime in the morning at that little house. There were half as many beds as there were us, and the pairing off was erotic and unexpected. Gathered mussels on the beach and made our supper. O'M sat in an armchair her head in her arms and heard records. I was the only one contented with the beach. Years later O'M still had a record, given her by Lori and inscribed "To the Huddled Armchair." That weekend started it, and it took a lot to make it stop again.

172

The image of that trip is the image of young girls standing naked in a small cabin, hair wet from the sea, examining each other for ticks, there were ticks on that beach. Like a Greek frieze in its innocence and beauty. Nothing had yet cracked down.

WACHET AUF on the radio here at Zeb's where I work late, perhaps all night, in the steaming heat of an August night, it is my birthday, or was till an hour ago, and I have for my thirty-first year just one resolve: namely, never to not drop anything that is in my hands when the words want to be written, babies, work, all, may they come crashing down about me, if so be it is necessary to sit at one of these abominable machines. Of where there are here so many, in so many colors. So many different types and shapes of machines sitting around me, some on blue desks and some on red, some on brown and some on green. Here where it grows very silent around 1 a.m. Even on a summer Friday night, which this is. One week before the August full moon. Papers and garbage and empty soda bottles gathered around me, the residue of a workweek. Different performance, but this was the cantata that lived in a purple envelope in my very first house, was it mine or Joan's, I wist not. A purple cover and torn, with the record scratched and played often. One of our favorite cantatas those years, the other being *Ich Hatte Viel Bekumneris*. But that I still have in its red cover and the duet, our favorite part, still playable. Did we not get that one from John Kaspar of ill fame, in his house on East Sixth Street around the corner from that first house of mine where I kept my records so orderly in that record cabinet beside the bed, manufactured as it had been (record cabinet, not bed) by one Buck Dunbar

173

whom I was in those days in the habit of "seeing," that is he was my lover, my first lover, full-fledged. I lay in that same large bed and lost my virginity, what was left of it, it went piecemeal, and listened to the rain falling on my fire escape and contemplated the fact that from then on I would be able to use Tampax with ease. An accomplishment I much desired. Buck I treated ill, and sent finally away. He returned drunk in the night to pick up the keys to his apartment on West Third Street, me in my bed not so much as turning over or speaking to him out of that darkness. The first Mexican food he bought me, and showed me many things he loved dearly, like the old rain gutters in the Village streets. A nest he had made, in the midst of books and built shelf-things, with dogs, and somewhere a young boy he was fond of, a son, who lived with a wife named Mike who made a Long Island scene full of cocktail parties with Djuna Barnes. A world he showed me, of austere license. "*Komm, kommst du - Ich komme*" singeth the German.

The taste of summer is the taste of dust and dampness and the smells of it thicken the blood here in the city where the summers of youth were the magic time, time of freedom, no one kept track of us or where we went. Joan and I passed many times that old movie theatre on Irving Place, long gone, where they showed *Blood of a Poet* for weeks on end, appalled and interested, not going in, it was years later that we finally saw it. The wind in Joan's hair as she buckled a belt on her jeans in the john at Washington Irving High School, where we studied geometry and English, where I wrote poems and met my first true love, a young young girl with heavy curling hair and thick lips, a girl named Pia Maria who took me home to her folks, and we listened all that summer to Puccini. Not Bach. This was before. Puccini, as we lay on sticky damp linoleum in that shack on Sheepshead Bay. An enchantment. Joan joined us, and Gloria, called then Mephistopheles, richness of woman in her, unresolved. An enthusiastic English teacher read my poems to the class. And arranged the meeting between Pia and me. The long trips on the subway to her house. The enchanted BMT with those dinky separate compartments, no subway cars like that anymore I imagine. The train went over the bridge, not through the tunnel. Allowing a certain rhapsody on Manhattan. Manahatta, my city, not mine anymore.

Those summers at Washington Irving full of privacy. A privacy I have never tasted since. NO ONE AT ALL knew what we were doing, at all. Our meetings in Union Square Park, our walks, all secret. The books we read summer after summer, the year that I read *Jane Eyre* a dozen times. Younger then, perhaps twelve, summer, held not even school. The freedom of sitting in endless luncheonettes, at endless drugstore counters and ordering lunch. The joys of a downstairs stationery store that was on a side street right near the school. Where we found notebooks, pens, to suit our works. A little old lady, long gone, I looked for the place last month as I walked by.

And after that the summers when I worked. Two of them. One in the mailroom of a factory. Made car parts in the building where I was working. Was it called Schroeder's? or what? I don't remember. Remember that I got $28.50 a week for a full-time day, but had fairly little to do. Spent much time writing and reading between the morning and evening rushes and rode around the factory in electric carts, all the guys giving me rides from office to office.

The next was an insurance office, which I hated. It was the next summer then. I think I was in college by then, or it was the summer before I left for college. One or the other. No, I was there. Did I not, from that job which paid thirty-five dollars a week, rush to meet Lori and O'M in the warm long twilights? Did I not, as much as I could, share that money with Lori? parents taking most of it "for college," leaving me a weekly allowance on which we subsisted. Yes, that was the same summer that we went to Boo's. On the Massachusetts waters which were not surf-y. And the summer before was the one of the great sadness. When we all realized that we must leave each other. Separate, set out for different colleges Pia Maria who stayed behind in the city, and Joan, and Gloria, and Audre, and Barbi Lutz who eloped without finishing high school, and Little One who did the same, it was said, with a white slave trader and was not heard from for years, tho when she did turn up it was only to be fat and wear a strange hat with feathers and look so sad and quenched and so from Queens, it was she who had carved "Save Yourself" on my bedspring and coined the then so beautiful phrase "I wanted it like I wanted myself..."

That summer of the sadness my parents took a vacation, the first that I can remember since the summers of my childhood, early childhood, a kind of summer that stopped when the war came, summers when I was three and four and we went to Long Beach and I saw what the sea was and felt it and Uncle Bill would take me out to where the water was over my head, holding me up and laughing, with the added mystery his bad hand in its glove gave his touch in my child's head. The night air when I snuck out of the house and went back out onto the beach, it was after dark, and the moon was full and quite high and I stood a long time looking at the water (the noises of the sea had called me out) and after a while a very fat man lying in the sand—his stomach sticking high into the air, almost level with my eyes—began to speak to me and I was telling him how I loved the night and the sea when my father appeared, upset, and took me home. After Long Beach there were summers—one or two? at a farm. Of which I do not remember as much, there was for me less magic there, but some, and especially in the barns there was magic. The smell of the hay and the smell of cows, which I still love, pulling a string I hadn't oughta have pulled and having a bundle of hay fall down on me, fall all over me, the smell, and the pieces of hay in my hair. Following brother Frankie who was just toddling out to the clover fields where the bees were, and losing our pail and shovel, walking till we reached the end of the farm. A barbed wire fence we looked thru, and another field with a bull in it. Corn huskings, an event, and sometimes outdoor fires. Tho it was not magic as the sea was magic, it had a beauty. And then the war came, we stayed home with our radios. There was no means of getting anywhere much, or else we had no heart for it, I don't know. I know it was cousins and uncles in Italy dying, and after a while we listened to the radio not at all, at least not while the children were up, and there were no newspapers all those years in the house which was a relief and cleared a space in my head which otherwise might have been filled with clutter. Goofy empty summers of going to Aunt Evelyn's, and having Cousin Chickie come to my house. Stickball in the Queens twilight, my futile attempts to learn to ride a bicycle (how I wrecked all the parked cars on the block) and the little Queens libraries in storefronts. Then the summer in typing school, when I spent every morning in a small room at Boro Hall and ambled back afterwards full of fff-ftf-frf-fgf-fvf-fbf, a game. Then the summers at Washington Irving, and the summers of work. And finally the summer when I had left home. The house on Fifth Street. The job on Wall Street. Lunches on the waterfront. Head taken over by Lori, a new kind of imagery in it, not cluttered, not rich, a little like having a demon. A world she lived in, like the world of Fifth Avenue mannequins in the store windows she loved so much. That we used to take the trip uptown to see. Whenever they had changed. An art, she made of that, and of the arrangement of rare furniture in a white room. Wherein I finally fell away from faith by painting my walls beige. Unnatural to me that austerity. Drinking rye in an open boat on the Sound in storms. Living on peanut butter and gin. Gristede's in New Canaan. A beautiful stark mystery, but it abandoned me. And left me to my own "abominable taste." I filled the house again with art nouveau busts and Italian cheese, gave up my job and school and began to model.

As I look back on them, I can understand why Alan so much hates summers. How much of them is spent suffering and waiting. Waiting for a promised phone call, or the return of someone who "just went out for a walk." But perhaps all this comes then because if it came to us in the Winter, in the grey and sunless time, it would not be endurable at all, not for an instant. Self-mutilation, the battering of the walls, the terrible scream we would send up from our cells, all this if the pain that comes to us in the heat came instead in the Winter.

The absolute taste of Pepperidge Farm whole wheat bread and cheese spread. And tomatoes. That summer when Lori shared my house for a while. (They are now playing the Opus 127 quartet, the SAME recording that I had that summer). The taste of that bread, that there was a truth to be gained somewhere in it, a perfect life to be led. Somewhere in it was Lori's love I was lacking. That I struggled so hard to gain. The night of the *festa* in Brooklyn when I walked with her for hours, her mouth twisted and sad and hard, not at all like those manne-quins she was—so short and so wide-hipped, and all that night she sang endlessly "Do not forsake me, oh my dar-ling," thinking of O'M whose terrible mother was at us. Somewhere in that bread was a great truth to be found. Or in the austerity of that small apartment. Ballet bar and piano, neat record holder made by Buck, with many compartments so the records wouldn't fall on each other, and the shelves, all orange crates, all filled with books. In that clean sad sanity and order, my filling up of time till that love should burst into blossom between us, as of course it never did. No love ever had that has not at once I think. We wait now, husband and I, for same miracle. The waters of Manhattan, and mosquitoes, and allergies, rush in to fill the vacuum we have made.

The next summer Lori was around, but less. I was not working full time and had less money to give her. I went to the Thalia a lot, carrying a bag of food and spending the day. Seeing the same Cocteau movies over and over. The same we had hesitated before five years earlier. *The Eternal Return*, *The Eagle with Two Heads*. Dwarves, magic, women with guns, the eternal black-robed goddess. Statues that wept and bled, long opium pipes. The wondrous lobby where I stretched out and ate.

Then seeing Lori years later at Mo's apartment, upstairs from my apartment on Houston Street. Mo had brought Jeanne upstairs without telling me. How sad and a little envious of my child she was. How long she talked to her. She was working in Stamford making electronic equipment. She was paying off her new Austin Healey. She was having an affair with one of the girls I knew—was it Felicia?

And other notes of Long Beach come to mind: a round table not much lower than my head. Or the same height. A bare wood floor that I looked at a lot. A couple of popular songs, bearing mystery to me in their very words. "*Bei mir bist du schoen*" and "Let Me Call You Sweetheart." The naps that the grown-ups always took on the beach: "just resting their eyes." The smell of citronella at the farm. On top of sunburn, and the sound of mosquitoes. The damp, green smell of that farmhouse.

Always it seems to me that I have not understood love. It was a thing that swept over the people I loved, and swept them away from me. (As for instance, away from our home on Morton Street, the furnished room with the tree outside, light in the leaves, and a lovely tiled bathroom, from which we were swept one night, Joan and I. We had spent the three days and nights before laughing and talking with a young man named Mike and O'Meara left with him and our house was gone.) Or it was a thing that swept over me and swept me away from right conduct and good living. From dharma, into things that made no sense. But never so often for me as for the others. The ones I loved and wished to grapple to my side. The ones whose fading voices on the wind I often hear at night while I am typing math for Zeb Delaire. In this strange bright loft on Eighth Avenue where I sit. Sadly and often I turned my eyes away. And I was embarrassed, I was embarrassed for them. Or mostly for them. Not wishing to see into their heads, or my own. Wishing that I could wish simply to be kissed. Tucked into bed as I once was by Cadena. Though my head told me love was a fine and splendid thing, my spirit told me other, and I mourned. I mourned our paths, the twistings of the way. As Freddie mourned for me when Roi first stayed.

Yes, this morning it was my birthday and I got up, went downstairs to the mail and remembered that no one would remember it was my birthday. A courtesy Freddie and I kept for one another. Last year the wooden altar that stands in my study. Fragile last work of his hands. So that today I pretended (finding a pink sleeveless polo shirt amongst his cast-off clothes) that Freddie had brought me a present after all. Tears in my head, in my answers all day to Alan. Who trotted oblivious to Brooklyn after his car. A chariot from which we shall see the North.

SONG FOR MY SPOOKS

Oh, my beloved spooks, I feel you gather about me
Strong as the wind, a breath always in my ear, loving
You who know to laugh at my pomposities, loving
You who support me in the dingy holes we will live in,
    the dark places
filled with grime and shadow, that will be ours now, I
    fear
Fill them with light, with spook laughter, light up the
    corners of the damp
with your loving, so that the words I write will echo
filled with more dimension, more past and future than
    they dream of yet
with the stardust of your hopes, the quick gestures of
    your dying
Fill my pillow with dreams, and give me the strength
    for our darkness
For this is the end of Kaliyuga, dark time on a dark
    planet
And I will not say I am not afraid or sad, make me strong
Find me a real flower or two for the children
Tell me stories as I scrub out our houses and make
    them larger
Sing to me softly as I cook our rice

Freddie lies by the record cabinet eating hardboiled
eggs. Keats sits by the window wrapped in a shawl, they
stand in the doorways, lean on the bookcases, filling
the air with shapes. They live in music. I am not alone.
In this setting forth I feel them, the wind that will carry
me out. It is easy, says Freddie, it only takes a minute
and it is done, you don't have to think about it. The
wind still in his hair. Alan says we must die soon but

l, I feel the weight of cauldrons of rice in dark houses, the fear and stealthy horror that creeps over the earth, that will fill it this autumn, and I wonder at this dark place in the midst of our bright adventure. The shape of being a pre-Homeric Greek, at the brink of a continent not yet explored or filled. In Wyalusing there are Indians living in wooden colonial houses, they till the land, they are waiting.

And now the tribe prepares to divide our estate. Whether we die or travel is not clear. No longer possible, a toehold on our rock. Manahatta, our poisoned rock— bad air, bad water. We wheel over it like gulls crying out against this. Against our forced migration. Green air solid and square like a square lime sherbet, a cloudy ice cube. The story of this summer is of a trip. Not yet begun, a long strange odyssey, a setting out not defined. Only last Fall it was we said LET IT COME DOWN, as it has been coming since, and on our heads. As then you fell, and took our house with you. Our House, in the old sense, dynasty, has fallen. And we are left, naked people on a rock. Seeking a dent, a hole to hide our cubs.

We have seen the houses of Brooklyn, the houses of Hoboken. The houses of Staten Island are hidden in trees. They are covered with mold and mildew, they are gentle. The houses of Tibet are the ones we seek. A long time coming. The houses of Rockland Maine look out at the sea. The people smile, the clothes and the food are cheap. There we ate homemade pie and bought sturdy shoes. We took a ferry to an island called Vinalhaven. Where the people are poor, the houses luxuriant. And neat, of another time, they face out to sea. They were the houses of fisherfolk, the houses of granite workers. We climbed like lizards in an abandoned quarry. The huge, cut stones lying idle in fields of moss. The green and white of lichens, the stone pink from the shells of millions of tiny beings. Sun cut thru a fog that was made of the sea itself. Thru an air that nourished as we breathed it in. We turned toward the south then, we stopped a night in Cambridge. We made our way to the mountains of Pennsylvania.

The houses of Pennsylvania are falling to dust. Oak furniture ninety years old rots in the rooms. The floors are strewn with the shells of greenish walnuts. Chipmunks and squirrels sport on the spindle beds. The barns of Pennsylvania are full of buckwheat. It rots, it is not bought or carried away. The land is rich, the people are very poor. The cows are smart, the people are rather mean. Niggardly toward animal and wife. The land has turned against them and they rot. Their buckwheat rots, their horses are fat and sloppy. Their wives are restless and take the children away.

The towns have beautiful names like Wyalusing. An Indian thrives there, he has a rather large farm. There are piles of stones on the hills almost as old as the hills themselves. For signal fires or for burial mounds? The corn was higher than anywhere else we'd been. The drought not so severe there as on the coast.

The houses of Pennsylvania are small. A ladder leads to the loft upstairs for sleeping. They are built like the barns, and the barns are built like the houses. The

Winters are long and very cold. The Susquehanna is a mighty river. It creeps now low between its drying banks. The barns of Pennsylvania are full of calves. That grow for ten weeks like cabbages and die. That want to get out, that want to see the sky.

The houses of Bedford-Stuyvesant stand in trees. Front yard and back, white pillars on their porches. We came to them thru the surly town of Wilkes-Barre. Thru the Greyhound terminal, and then thru subways. We found pleased, gentle Black folk, Jamaicans on porches, too many watchdogs, wind in the high city. The boats and the river looked back at us where we stood. The el on Myrtle Avenue roared by. Pratt students with long flat hair ate hamburgers. We found a home there, but it turned against us. A house of wood and brick, gas fireplaces. An art nouveau house of wall fixtures and gardens, in which we could have lived, but we turned aside. Not moving swiftly enough, and it slipped away. And we are left lost and naked on our rock.

The houses of Manhattan are grey with soot. Dirt, pigeon droppings, ashes, are the patina. The people squint against the cinders in the wind. They look at you kindly, they are smart and quick. Backyards are full of gravel and broken pavement. Food dropped from windows rots under ginko trees. Cats play in the long weedy grasses, as do children.

September 18. It is Indian summer, the fall is upon us, but a hot wind blows down the length of the island, down thru the avenues that cut it in strips. Is it the last moon we shall see from this island, this Indian summer, the leaves are already dropping. Last year they did not drop till the end of October. Till after you died. Now they are dropping already. I sit in my shop, it is cool, the water is dripping as always in the bathroom, my drunk landlord stopped by but I had no rent, the patterns and shadows of ten or twelve years of living. Determined by *La Vie de Boheme*, by the smoked herring and Coca-Cola of our youth. Determined by the gods and ghosts we had conjured. The *Francesca da Rimini* of Tchaikowsky, the *Manfred*, *Prometheus Unbound*, *Thus Spoke Zarathustra*. But slowly over the past twelve years a shadow has been growing over these colors. The glory of poverty is not enough. (Tho I am in love with obscurity, with an unknown Roi Jones buying pears on First Avenue, a humble Beethoven washing out his socks.) We have set out, we are heading toward the sea. Away from the poisoned waters. We seek a resting place. Out of these shadows, how they grow. They grew as I sat on the stoop one summer day, the steps of an unknown house in the Village, was it on Twelfth Street, were we on our way to the New School? There where I sat with Lori who had bought a paper and we read that the Rosenbergs had been executed. "That's the beginning of the end," said Lori. Which had been said before, and in the summer. Summer's a time of doom and of bliss, always one or the other, I remember one of my birthdays, my father coming home late, there was the war, we were waiting for him before we cut the cake and he came in and threw down a newspaper with headlines one hand high, we had bombed Hiroshima. "Well, we've lost," he said, "whatever we do now we've lost." We cut the cake, my brothers were wearing hats.

It is in summer that we feel these shadows. Their creeping over our lives, the making of greys. The lack of light as the forest grows over us. Today China is marching to the Indian border.

The richness of summer eludes me, I pursue it. The richness of all the summers of my life. The heat and stillness of air, the grasshoppers busy. The cobalt skies behind the moving trees. The park with my grandfather in the soft green dusk. The tales he told the other night wanderers. The magic in the West 80s, off the park, the all-night radios and phonographs pouring out loud Latin rhythms on the street, the people dancing, children up all night. The sleepy Black children at 2 a.m. getting on the Fourteenth Street crosstown to Avenue D, cotton candy still in their hands and in their mouths. The rhythms of city summer have left me, perhaps forever. The lazy grace and indulgence of those times. As I had always known them. Movies and notebooks, parks and candybars. Malted milks. I live now on rice. Goodbye, malted milks. Goodbye, l-t-down-mayo in luncheonettes, aircooled, with high turning stools where we practiced "spotting" for ballet class. They are not even aircooled anymore, because our rock is running out of water.

I grasp at it, I try to get it down, to make you a present of it, the summers we'd known. The summers you shared with me and the ones you didn't. The one when you took off and we saw you no more till the fall. Gone back to Ossining probably, to try and cut loose. Of this life that was turning you back to an archetype. Back to the victim, eternally, so that you wept for it. But they elude me still, the essence of them. Was it that I was free then to come and go? To hitch all night and day on the old Post Road, to sleep under stars, steal corn and sleep in quarries. Free to make any choice until I had made some choices. And then it vanished, the summer I carried Jeanne. One choice that carried all the rest inside it, like those carved ivory balls in Chinatown, nested inside each other and not to be removed.

The summer I woke and discovered I was not free was 1958. I have fought long against this. I come to accept it now, I head for the sea. Bearing my children and books, to study necessity and harmony. But in 1958 Jeanne was a baby, I noticed that I could not always go out, that I could not hitch thru New England or spend whole days at the Thalia. That I could not head for Central Park in the morning, my notebook under my arm and wait out the day there reading and writing and wandering by the lakes. I noticed for the first time where I was living. That I had bartered the space and smokestacks and riverwind and rats for a few small rooms and roaches on Houston Street. Which used to be a swamp and had been filled in. The sky no longer visible, a study in depth began. A history of rebellion against my fate. Against what I had chosen. Deliberate search for amusement, the work sat patiently waiting to be discovered. To be enacted. Sat with its tail curled softly around its feet in the corner of my desk where it sits still. But now gets up to cavort time and again. To do a little dance on the desk by itself.

In 1958 I lived in my house. Jeanne went away for a time, to Greenwood Lake where my mother sat her in carriages and brushed her hair. I went to the movies with Cubby and A.B. On Fourty-Second Street we'd stop at Grant's, and I would eat fried clams. There was a carnival across from my house on the side of Houston where houses had been. The houses had gone, a road was going thru but so far there was only a carnival and carnie folk nightly in the neighborhood bar where I went with Howie Schulman. They offered us a job running the Ferris wheel, they needed someone, spoke of a Winter traveling thru the south, and again I realized I was not free, there were no choices my first child had been born.

I spent two weeks with Howie while Jeanne was at Grandma's. In his parents' purple and satin silly house. We dined on tuna fish and took long walks. One night I remember we sat in a half-built house in the middle of an empty lot and we were talking about nothing in the dark when bright lights came on at us from all directions and a voice said "All right, come on out of there!" We did—it was many cops pulled up at both ends of the building and shining their headlights into its airy spaces. The fear and anger making the shadows longer.

In 1959 I lived with Zella. Although I still had my house and stayed in it. You stayed in it too bringing home hundreds of boys. You went away for a while to summer stock. I believe that Mo and Pauli lived upstairs. That you came home from stock with a swollen ankle, having badly sprained it doing a dance you hated. That Felicia at that time was in your bed where she had been left by Lee Forrest, a beautiful junkie, she brought Felicia there one evening, carried her in and laid her first on Mo's bed upstairs, saying to me "Sweetie run up every fifteen minutes and see if she's still breathing." Tried to teach me on the spot to give salt injections. I wondering what the hell to do with a corpse. Felicia breathed, recovered, threw up a lot. Demanded ginger ale which I went and bought. Devoured that, threw up, and went downstairs. She fell down most of the way but would take no help. Fell out in your bed and slept for two days and nights. While you wired me from somewhere you were coming home. And I went out to meet you and your torn ankle leaving Felicia in the hands of three or four friends. All lovely, worried young dykes who talked a lot.

That summer I often would cross to Avenue C and walk to the studio Zella kept on Sixth Street. A tiny room, hardly big enough to stand in: disconnected refrigerators, stoves, old Spanish chairs, black wood, boxes of pins, neatly labeled. In a larger room to the side where some packing crates with a pillow served as a bed I would lie and watch Zella paint, sometimes till dawn. In her faded blue sweatshirts, her constant trying to get hold of a life, the labeling of paint, numbering of casein colors. Her eyes an incredible blue like the dawn from her sixth-floor window, her shoulders enormous, her breathing an incessant wheeze, she would lay one tone of blue beside another tirelessly, or we would go out for coffee at Johnny Miller's all-night greasy spoon, sitting among the gossip laid out by Ruthie the waitress whose son had quit college, who was having a baby. One night instead we went to Frankie & Charlie's, another luncheonette one block away, they had tables, which Johnny Miller's didn't, but the english muffins were stale and there was no gossip. This night (there had been a heat wave for a week) a napkin fight suddenly broke out among the blue formica tables between a bunch of the local gangsters and the "regulars" who were five or six streetwalkers from Avenue D. Zella and I sat there in the black and steaming heat and watched a score of the toughest of the neighborhood cavort with shouts and squeals, duck behind tables, while Charlie stood behind the counter expressionless and watched the fun. It was a hot and brooding summer and after a while when I went up Avenue C to Zella's house I began to notice the children were being pulled in early, there were streetlights broken out for a stretch of two or three blocks, plunging whole areas into darkness, and one night when I walked that six-block stretch and found Zella out I got into a cab for the return trip because the hairs on the back of my neck, the jungle instinct that develops when you grow up in a city, told me that to walk those blocks again, and so soon, would simply not be cool.

These last two summers have been punctuated with a new kind of noise, a kind of siren that the New York police have added to the list of the horrors that they inflict on the city. A wa-wa-wa kind of noise, the first time that Mini heard it she was standing in our kitchen, her eyes got very big and she said, in resignation and jungle fright: "Here comes *another* elephant."

In the summer of 1960 I did penance. In the late spring of that year I aborted our baby, the only son Roi & I are likely to have, and in the reconciliation that followed I sought him out or waited for his call which never came when it should have. Would come in the dead of night, in some kind of desperation. I had the phone on my wall near the kitchen, miles from the bed, and would stagger over to it in the dark, and yes, he could come up, okay, and it would start again. But for weeks on end, our having made some summer plan, some place we could go and be together, I waited and no call came and I would think on the child I might be growing big with.

The following summer was easier, I was working. In Larry Wallrich's bookstore. The young men came and went, with dope, with guns. All like a John Wieners poem. LeRoi was sick, arrested, I had sent Peter Hartman away. I went to San Francisco. I remember the walk across New York the morning before I left, I had been all night with Larry in the store, cocaine and emotions had overtaken us. I set out at dawn to go home across Houston Street and heard the cooing of pigeons in a building. Looking closely, I saw the building, it was one that had been partly shattered the day before by the wrecking ball that hung in the air next to it. I realized them in that stillness and soft light, and watched the ball swaying slightly in the wind.

       That morning I stopped in a church on West Houston Street run by Franciscans and heard part of the six o'clock mass. The girls from the streets in their bright dresses and hats were easily distinguished from the respectable women, mostly in black with black kerchiefs on their heads, their dresses to the floor. And I stepped out into a morning on the stone church steps, a full-blown morning with bustle and the smell of provolone and the smells of Sunday pastries, *cannoli* and *sfogliatella*, mingling in the air, and watched the women in black go down those stone steps and remembered all this from other lives and times, re-membered Italy where I have never been.

Which I found to some extent in San Francisco. The cream-colored houses tumbling up the hills, the high clear air and the harbor. Mike McClure's house, like some house in Bayside, Long Island, the wood and the trees outside bending, bending in the wind, peering in the bay windows. Jay De Feo painting upstairs, her huge rose thick on the wall. Turtles and lizards striding about the rooms, and Mike like any one of us, selling everything, preparing to embark for the enchanted city. New York, where they held out two months and then returned. The beautiful tables and armchairs moving out, Kirby Doyle carting armloads of things off into the woods. Larkspur, where I stayed a few days with him and DeeDee. Reading Walt Whitman and making friends with the trees. Met there George Herms in a lit-tle house on the mudflats. Surrounded as always with sculptures hanging in trees. Paintings on the side of his house, inside one sat on sculptures, ate off them, the Herms baby pulled herself up and walked by the aid of them. There, at a Nuisance Party given by George, for George, for that he was being thrown off his mudflat as a Public Nuisance, a menace to the health and mor-als of the mudflats, I watched long skinny girls nursing healthy babies, I watched the ones of the earth eating free figs from the abandoned orchards of San Rafael, and wondered at the fear that had led me to an abor-tion. And decided to come home and have Roi's baby, whether he liked it or not. There in that space and ease, that climate of plenty, it all seemed not only possible but easy. And so I came home, catapulted back a week

193

before I intended and slept with Roi again on the eve of his trial, the night of my return, and there in the hashish smoke on my foam rubber couch made Mini.

The McClures soon followed me east as they had planned, they were here the first week of September, and found a house on East Fourth Street that I later inherited. Janie and Jeanne spent mornings and afternoons together with Janie's turtles and Jeanne's paints. Kyra hated New York and went to bed. As I was to do, a year and a half later, in Topanga.

(Have just been out walking, selling books in the hot grey streets of the city. The Village Art Show flat and depressing as always clogging the streets with innumerable women too big for the slacks they're in strolling slowly by talking to ARTISTS, all the paraphernalia of the Village in the beginning of fall, now performed under circumstances of inhuman airlessness. Johnny Dodd and Charles on the steps of the house where you died. I wonder if they now sit there without any consciousness of that, is it a comforting thing like having the family cemetery on your own property. Happy and covered with shades of various design, they strolled to Joe's Diner where I used to meet Nicky Thacher and ordered Pork Chops and Spaghetti.

Walked back, nine dollars the richer for our books.)

In the summer of 1962 I had had Mini. She nursed at me and I lay in bed and read. I had a breast infection and high fever, I went to my mother's house and recovered a bit. Translated Latin poems and looked out the picture window at the Lake. That had a mountain behind it that hit you in the eye. Looming green thing, and the speed boats zooming by. I nursed the child, other people took care of it. Other people changed it and rocked it while I wrote. Typed envelopes for Orientalia Books in the evenings. Out of a huge directory of the world. Played records, read *Moby Dick*, feared to return. Returned at last to the city, it was in August. The bus ride in, I was terrified knowing I had at last bitten off more than I could chew. That this baby in my arms was one too many. This and Jeanne and I could not feed them or care for them. That I simply was not strong enough for it. And dreamed that night of a young man come to fetch me. Come to take me away to live with him, Roi was dying. Roi was not dying, he came to sit by my bed. Speechless, almost daily, he held that small mite in his arms. Love burned between us. Then Alan moved in and we went to Fire Island. To a strange little house Michael Malce had at the Pines. Right next to the taxi stand and grocery store. Where we stayed a week, all four of us very happy. Nearly burned the place down burning massive driftwood in the potbellied stove. Mini slept wrapped in her blankets on the beach while we climbed the dunes, walked miles, and came alive. On our return we set out, that time for the West.

In 1963 we returned to the city. Found you and DeeDee Doyle living with John Daley on Fifth Street. Two doors from Johnny Wieners. We holed up in Clive's pad, a house behind a house on Avenue A. Thence found our way to 35 Cooper Square. And the Hearth. Dust was rife, the air full of falling plaster, the summer of Birth of Alex. My Leo son. Long days in the hospital looking at the East River. How it made waves in the wind against its banks. Long days of writing letters, recovering. Flowers from Edwin Denby. Nurses that came in the night to take my blood pressure. Every hour, all night long, for fear I should die. For that I bled so much.

My long time in that white room with the eave, our bedroom at Cooper Square. Recovering and sleeping. Alan pulled up nails all summer from the floorboards. Played in Jack Smith's movie in Old Lyme, Connecticut. Fullbellied, awaiting Alex. Danced on a pink cake twelve feet in the air. *Normal Love*, in the open air under the greeny trees. And the evenings there in the barn, gay circus creatures sewing sequins on their costumes under the beams in the high silences.

The summer of '64 George ushered in. By flying back, at eclipse of the full moon, back to his woods and out of the Big Apple. Leaving us with a task which was more than we could manage without him. Leaving us to the joys of the opulent tower.

That is the summer that's left to write of now, the last we spent together, your apartment on Ridge Street we named the Opulent Tower.

The darks of the opulent tower when it was nighttime. The summer night we spent talking together—in that other room while Alan and Kirby were exploring *The Blossom* and Alan was shedding skin after false skin. You and I hid in the kitchen drinking coffee, you had the mug Jeanne made you, you told me you were going to die soon, it was the last night of *Home Movies*. I looked at you and wondered if it was true. Not knowing it then, not knowing it till that fall, till the day before your death when we spoke at Coscia's sitting at that one red formica table I still sit at most often and drinking eternally coffee which I now cannot swallow or I shall die soon. You and I in the dark made magic that night. It was August and very still, the church across the yard had stopped singing, no one extra was there, just you and I and Kirby and Alan, and we were talking in twos. I called up for you a little of the light, a little of the power I was exploring and pressed my palms to your forehead, you drank it in. I don't remember what we said, I do remember that our love for each other was complete, that it had come at last to rest, that we rested in each other and leaned on the tub in the kitchen and talked and talked. So much has left since then, not only you, but you, and coffee, and schmattas, and satins, and richness, and all the life of the flesh, its opulence, and you and the reds and blacks of little theatres, their amber lights and greens, and left to me now is the sea, and brick and wood, and the hope of healing thru peace and discipline, and the hope of growing thru study and breathing, the hope of air somewhere. And gone is Manahatta, the tall city, and Kirby's flown away with all his songs. Debbie came and took the schmattas out of my house, she is very brave, she is trying to make a nest. The streets are seething, they are violent, they break out here and there with pustule shouts and agony of grey. Heat, cold, it is all one, it is grey, it is grey here, how can we bear it, even the three weeks that are left before we leave. The dirt and bitterness. The people who remain here, waiting to die. The water fluoridated and turning brown. The air a poison gas. They with distended bellies and bowed legs. Children like those in CARE pictures after the war. Herbert Huncke looking like a refugee. Debbie took the blue satin schmatta that I got you out of the Becks' house when they flew the coop a year or more ago. The morning that Kirby and I spent up there, among schmattas and ruins, among the costumes, the endless theatre pictures. I found thirty dollars on the floor and we ate a lot. Kirby shot up, tying up with a black velvet strip he found in Judith's bedroom. We rode downtown with our arms full of broken watches, and pieces for your tent on the Ridge Street roof. Presents for Arione, for Dale and Elsene. And now Arione is in Europe and moving east, and Dale awaits trial and jail for selling pot, and Elsene is hiding in Brooklyn working a lot, saving money and promising herself she'll move one day. SPLAT! "Industry's growing, all thru the Maritimes." I cling to the hope that the sea will be the same. That there in the north we can live and make books. Blue air, like the blue of the dawn in the opulent tower. The run we took to the river, Kirby and I, hand in hand as the light broke. Is the river there still, haven't seen it in a year. I know it is there because Jeanne came home in tears from yesterday's school, she nearly got pushed into it. I expect you will come and live with us by the sea. I expect you will get into the child we make. On LSD in Vinalhaven I saw that you had melted into Alan, that you had (partly) taken over his flesh, curious and greedy.

fall

OCTOBER

I stand here in my shop in the rain in a place of transit. The house is behind us. There is a new bright padlock on the door, work of an evil man who fears to be robbed. Who made us homeless. Who gave us a new home. At the shop at the back are boxes piled to the ceiling, the shop itself is the wagon for setting out. I feel the sway and pull and we go forward.

Loneliness overtakes us one and all. In the rain at this end of a year of evil omens. Explicit events slowing down the roulette wheel. I dreamed of Freddie, he told me he was having a concert at Judson. He was triumphant about it. I try to remember last year at this time. I remember nothing but an impending disaster. I remember too the nursery rhymes I read. One Wednesday night after the other, at the round table.

> Oh that I were
> Where I would be
> Then would I be
> Where I am not
> But where I am
> There must I bide
> And where I would be
> I cannot
> AND WHERE I WOULD BE I CANNOT.

In my dream you were triumphant about your concert. In Alan's dream you were tired, you invited him to come and live with you and he agreed. This is a different day but it is the same. The same rain falling out of the same sky. The same old tired rain. Try to picture its color when new "when the world was new," the silver color of rain, the light in it. Yes, it is October in an empty city. Tired town and yet last night, the full moon rising as it did over the towers of Manhattan, I stood at a window in the Dakota at Seventy-Second Street, stood looking out over the park and saw here the epitome of THE CITY. In the sport of the Mother who builds up and pulls down, trying combinations one after the other of cities, the towers of Babylon, of Athens, of Istanbul, of Benares, of Vladivostok, of Kiev, the risen and fallen Thebes, Carthage, magic names, shape after shape the sculptress has tried and abandoned, this one of the closest to the word "city" with A PAPER MOON rising over it waits to be pulled down, this one of the closest because one of the last, the Kaliyuga hissing around us like an almost spent fuse, the children dancing in our drab hotel, glad, glad to be alive and singing at dawn. I wonder at them, I wonder at myself as I cook their rice, the singing in me. Which is: his bellybutton might close tomorrow, as Jeanne reminded me yesterday, speaking of Vishnu. So be it. *Docet*. It is fitting. What more pleasure?

Last year, three days before your death, did you, under constraint and complaining the while, help me to carry firewood home to The House, that which was for us epitome of House, while I explained to you how important the fire was and urged you on, bitching. Did you then desire to whisk Jeanne from her duties into a day of play, you both together instead took dance class, I insisting it was important that Jeanne take dance class. Now on the radio is *La Boheme*, belonging to an unspeakably ancient layer of myself. And I wonder a lot about the lost cities of Africa, how the Mother fashioned them and if they pleased her. I am sure that Manahatta pleased her a while, it was so willing to play, to sport in the incandescent glow of Maya. And then, drooping like John Cage in the sixties, like an old fire just before dawn, like pumpkins caught in a frost, it lies now grey, the towers are melting, they are flattening out, they are almost not there at all. WHERE THERE WERE TOWERS ARE NOW FLAT OFFICE BUILDINGS. Melting like wax, the spires of Manhattan in the heat of approaching events. The river turns black, it turns back on itself, it fills with salt. There is a fire waiting under the earth. Under the earth's skin. So that we dance more lightly, leaping into the air. Harvey Brown in Buffalo makes books. I make books. John Wieners, Olson hiding in Gloucester reads (maybe) the hymns to Kali John got from me. Eleven million Turks are voting today, the man on the radio just said to me. Truly, wonderful is the sport of Brahma.

I bow before the rain in the windy streets. I whisper a last goodbye to my long-gone house. To the broken wall in the kitchen where someone long before us looked for a fireplace. To the wooden floors that bit at high heels, that gave way unexpectedly beneath us. To the oval window in the closet that opened onto nothing but the hall. To the red white and blue of the nursery, the blue wall I painted last year, the windows cracked and too dirty to see out of where Alex and Mini would sit day after day calling down to the street below them. To the stairs. To the angle of the stairs. The endless perilous journeys I took on them, on LSD, their unbelievable steepness. To our bedroom where the traffic became the sea. Where I could hear goats grazing, and the seawind. The roof and glorious wall where I meditated. Or read Milarepa. To the eave thru which snow drifted, endless snow, falling so softly into our wooden room. To the entrance into the void which I have closed, so that our house, which was and is one of the Hearths, shall not be moved, or opened, in our time. To the ghosts of the Indians who used to live there. To the stove, whose pipe fell out just before we left, where I burned papers in the Wintertime. To the skylight in my study that rained onto my bed. The magic solemn bookcases, now painted black, now filling a store on West Eighty-Ninth Street, holding new books belonging to no one at all. To my good round table, where readings were and feasts, under that big yellow lamp, two years of feasting. All gathered together in that golden light, the quick and dead, the good and the treacherous, the fat and thin, bald heads and heads of hair, Mini biting the edge of the table, or scratching it, Jeanne polishing it with lemon oil on Saturdays. How it opened up for the solstice feasts is a story too. Freddie and John Worden gobbling pig and turkey. Merce eating beef stew in wine with LaMonte and A.B. Friends in a friendly time, we were young enough, still, for that. The various moods of the fireplace. Red door that nothing could break down, covered with dents and splinters. Police lock that didn't work, ridiculous eyehole. Lights that did not work, good fat hot water heater. Also not working. Delightful Winter mornings. Hermses in springtime, wrecking everything. Roof full of mint and begonias, broken skylights. Thru which Alex would drop an occasional shoe.

And now, some nights later, moved to a hotel. My fat red typewriter stands on a hotel desk. Safe in this curtained room and I want to write of the sounds outside on Broadway. The lack of rain this fall. The clear high air. As I remember fall, not as last year was. The leaves are gladly coming down in the park. The children sport in them when I take them out. Rejoicing in the combining of the elements, all the elements as one, sky ground air trees all covered with the same brown brittle leaves. They throw them up again as they come down. Throw them up to meet their brothers in the falling. The fall was named for this phenomenon. And Mini picks up acorns, Alex chases pigeons, the light is strong and good, the wind is cold. IT IS AS I REMEMBER NEW YORK IN THE AUTUMN. A clear delightful thing. The city I say goodbye to.

To the A train, full at night of stoned Black ladies in green dresses and fake mink capes, leaning against their men as the train rolls that long run from 59th Street to 125th. To the heavy brooding air that is there now. Sharp tension. To the bums, the children and cats which will be removed, to the Mott and Broome Streets which they will tear out, no more the fish stores, strange good Mafia restaurants with no menus, where they "charge what the traffic will bear." To the shape of the Brooklyn Bridge (I thought today of buying it on a postcard to take along). We look a lot at the map of Nova Scotia. Conjuring a house. On the cliffs near Ingonish, looking out at the sea. A huge stone house and barns and rolling fields. Horses for Alan and Jeanne, a kitchen garden. Pantries and root cellars, large stone fireplaces. Incredible air, long Winters, springs full of flowers. Closets and closets of blankets, made of good wool.

The children sleep, Jeanne on a mat on the floor. A sleeping bag we got her for her birthday. The subway goes by outside under Broadway. It reverberates between the high stone walls of these buildings. Walls on which the sun sets much as it sets on mountains. Walls which after thirty-one years I am leaving. For other cliffs on which the sun will set.

Perhaps we shall see icebergs out to sea. (I cannot look backward tonight, cannot say goodbye.) I know we shall see the aurora borealis. Sea creatures unknown here, other colors, a color of sea I have never seen. Those long black nights, sun rising at 10 a.m., the explosion spring will be. The treasures that are my library piece by piece. My learning how to weave.

And today saw Mike Strong escaped from two madhouses. Received again the message they all bring: "You must never let them catch you, if they catch you they cannot control their anger." Mike's hair still short, almost shaved, the years dropped out by shock that he doesn't remember. Same message as Kit Marlowe, Thomas Kyd, Joan of Arc. Gnostics and Albigensians. All those happy, mystic Spanish Jews. Same message always. JUST DON'T LET THEM CATCH YOU IN THE FIRST PLACE.

Though they are good and well-meaning, these New Yorkers. Manhattanites with quick eyes, tight mouths, a sense of humor. Grey people in a grey air, putting up with it. With the noise, the dust, with each other, on this island. "Fluoridation is poison, is treason, is in New York" says the sign at the place where I sometimes go to eat. I wonder how much further you would have come in a year. How much more you would have shed. It gets close to the time of year when you did your dance. I send a mass card to your family. Your silly family of which I know not what members and what genders still live in that house. I try to get Bobby Ossorio to take us to visit your grave. Where they have set up no stone. Out of some kind of reticence or shame. The stories they tell of your last visit home. How you threw out the furniture, set a mattress on the ground, surrounded yourself with mirrors and little boxes, and went to sleep for days. Which was enough to convince them that you were mad.

Now Tompkins Square Park where we walked has been torn up. It is handball courts and a bandstand, no more ghosts can walk its circular paths. And they have torn up the park where we sat with John. Alan, John Wieners and I, a symmetrical open block with diagonal paths. Stone benches without backs, simple, an open space. Where we sat one night, speaking of Cairo, speaking of love. Where I lay in the sun recently, amid their building. And found that the clouds were still moving across the sky.

And the cloths that you left behind are scattered at last. A year in the scattering. Schmatta trunk dispersed. Some schmattas at Debbie's, the rest left outside in the street, where the bums had the picking of them. I sit here in your shirt, a striped velour thing, the sleeves are so long on me I don't need potholders, just slip them down over my hands, it is a warm good shirt and I wear it a lot. Not everything has vanished. Not the smell of the air in Ossining, with the seeds blowing over your grave, the wind from the river, the smells of the burning leaves, That will not vanish, perhaps, till the earth passes.

But the coffeepot that we sat around together has wended its way to my mother's, she will fix it, replace the broken top by writing to Ecoware somewhere far away and ordering another. A household lady full of household order. I don't drink coffee now, or sit in the long afternoons with friends. I walk in the brisk air from the hotel to the shop, a somewhat brittle existence. The elevator (one of the two) says Suck Me. The bar downstairs full of dykes and gangsters, almost a throwback to the old Swing Rendezvous. The sewing machine beside the schmatta box, on which Louise used to sew, has been sold to the sad girl who bought our dying house. Which will fall in or burn down around her. While we swim away thru the empty air to our island. Or peninsula, to start with. Our round table sits at the Metro, waits to be sold. At which we kept the Solstice. Sold the pictures and pipes, scattered the jewels and trinkets. My one real jewel, green necklace, stolen away. I wear Tibetan skull round my neck, carved from the fingerbone of a long dead sage.

Today walked past Cooper Square and saw outside our house the boxes piled high, Peter Agostini's bushes and hanged man crushed in the top one, if I had not been with Alan I might have stopped, might have culled thru like any Bowery bum, looking for some treasure left from that old life. Like the black cutout men that Jeanne made me. The wondrous collages I left behind on the walls. A period of her life crushed out of shape. Unfindable. Ghost of Alan in the study hurried me always, did not allow me to pack what I should have packed. I wonder at myself for leaving that wall. Her "gallery" she called it. "Witchpins" the name of one magic collage left there.

Now the faucet drips in the kitchen, as the faucet has always dripped in the kitchen of every place I've lived since I left school. This morning walked out onto Broadway and smelled the smells of school campuses, the burning leaves, the crisp air, and realized how happy I had been at school and for those things only apart from the meddling and nudging that went on and I thought that if it were now I would figure out how to stay, just to keep breathing that acrid leaf-burning air in the fall, and the pear blossoms in the spring. But then the people meant more to me than the smells, than the wind from the river behind the woods, or the meadow full of wildflowers, and the long library stacks shaded and dusty. The people meant more and I followed them on their way. A thing I wonder at now, as I seek landscape.

We have pulled away from it, shed it in this year. Or as Lori wrote me then, too soon, not true: WE GO TO OUR OWN, YOU AND I, ASSAULT OF SUBSTANCE, ALTHOUGH IT IS NOT SUCH A HAPPY TIME. I have pulled loose, and you, come clear. Trees shelter me, they do not close me in. No claustrophobia, no fighting against it now. That the sea should be just outside, green underfoot. Trees and a large stone house.

At Raphael Soyer's there is a canvas of the Lower East Side, an "East Village" painting, I am walking out of the left side of the canvas, one hand in a pocket, ladies with babies lounge against walls, Allen Ginsberg stands among them with a peaceful look on his face.

I keep hearing the violin my father used to play. After work in the evening in our Brooklyn house, not the one we owned and lived in for so long, an earlier house on First Place, rented apartment, funny checkered linoleum in the kitchen on which I used to make parades of rubber toys, a bedroom with a frosted glass door thru which I continually expected a tiger to jump, breaking the glass and devouring me. And the violin in the small living room, green rug on the floor, large wooden radio in the bookcase. Radio on which we later heard the first war news. Daddy would play while Mommy sewed or read. LONG YEARS AGO. IN OLD MADRID. With great pauses, much vibrato. I wonder when the music in our family will wend its way into the light. In Alex, or one of my grandchildren, or when Alex laughing with total glee while Don Bas played his flute, one of the last nights at the round wooden table. Don, who remembers riding with Genghis Khan.

And the green floor at Vincent's house on Avenue A. You painted it green, to look like grass, wanting then underfoot what I go to seek out now. Always aware that trees weren't enemies. And yet you never managed to clue me in.

OCTOBER 26

Oh, it is bright today, the October sun! I follow your odyssey like a new Good Friday throughout this sunny week. So grey last year. Sunday was new moon, Kali's night. She sits on your altar now and blesses me. A year ago Sunday did Alan and I take the LSD on which we foresaw a tremendous setting out, pronouncing the words "Let it come down" resigning our posts as one of the two poles that held up this continent (the Bermans balancing on the other side). That LSD trip with my jeweled brick meditation wall followed by two days yours with Debbie Lee. When you saw that you had indeed destroyed your House. When you saw you were indeed the king who dies. When you came out of your curtained separate room and gently for hours taught Debbie what you knew. Making her lie down, teaching her every muscle. As she so sadly now recalls, and grateful. Now knowing then your decision, it comes clear you knew it, we went on. Lightly resigning a task too heavy for us. Telling each other the Apocalypse had already happened. As indeed it had in your seeing. We went blithely on. The moon was full. Harvest moon. At Wednesday reading, at the round table, the oracle Splitting Apart, "THERE IS A RIPE FRUIT STILL UNEATEN" it said, and we still did not see.

Day after the LSD I went out to gather wood with Jeanne. From a house full of pumpkin rinds and harvest foods. Met you near the construction site where the wood was and you carried huge timbers home for me on your shoulders, grumbling, wanting to come up and use the phone. Alan asleep, I hurried you out again, tho you could have used a shower and a nap. These simple human things, done wrong a thousand times, the bed refused, or the towel, the dollar not offered, this time take on the reverberations of thunder. This time fill up the sky with a cloud of blood. You wandered out again and played with Jeanne. Took class with her, gave her an amulet (which Debbie Lee has lost). I, filled with the sorrows of our future departure so clearly revealed while tripping, the clear bright skies so cold, the stars of different colors, leaning against Alan in a wagon which traveled and traveled over end-

211

less plains, cold, silent, looking backward in my heart, all this revealed, I, filled with these sorrows, gave you no second thought. The king who would trigger it off. SO IT HAS ALWAYS BEEN WITH ORACLES. That day, there was a ripe fruit still uneaten.

You wandered on, thru an unspeakable odyssey. You seem to have been everywhere at once. Last year today, it was a Monday then, you called and told me all your friends were busted. Thru something you had inadvertently said. You told me they had killed all the children in the world. The streets were empty. I told you get some sleep. "You know I think I'll never sleep again." There was wonder like a child in your voice. I asked you out for coffee. I asked Alan to get up (unprecedented) and come with me. We met you in Coscia's, at the corner table. Last time I ever saw you. We had coffee. We talked, you listened a lot, about the setting out, about the apocalypse being over, about picking up now, shards on the beaches, pieces of the shattered world just past to build a new one with. You said not everyone would make it thru. No I said and I looked you in the eye, I knew you were thinking of yourself, but did not foresee the event— but they will make the bridge and they will be back again. You took it at that. You said we made you happy. You said all the people in the street were crying "except the Puerto Ricans, they know where it's at." You stole my flute, and then you went away.

That night a phone call asking me to a party. To the roof of Ridge Street, the old opulent tower. To which I never went. I was to bring the *The Calculus of Variation* to read. You would dance. You would make a dance "to

212

conjure Kirby Doyle." To bring your Black Irish brother back to the city. No one came but Johnny Dodd and Debbie Lee. And you sent her away. All night, a wandering, a to and fro. Ralph di Padova, a hood or undertaker, driving you everywhere in an old black Pontiac. Your Passion. That you rode the elevator in Andy Warhol's building up and down for hours in the night.

In the day (tomorrow) you met Johnny Dodd and went home with him for a shower. You cleaned yourself, you danced, you shed your flesh. A leap that bought the new age, and turned us loose.

And the other day sitting in a movie with Alan I watched him become excited and like a child about a beautiful barn on the screen and I thought suddenly and lightly for the first time in a year how young we were. The ILLUSION of our youngness overcame me, I almost felt American, I thought of barns and cars and horses and young children, and lightly, lightly, I touched my husband's arm. But as we got up to leave in the dark, the cloak of our true age, the number of times we have done these things, the infinite number of your deaths, settled on my shoulders again, a magic cloak that nothing will remove. I felt the age I feel in yoga class, in all my prayer and study and lost again—so fast—that timid glorious western illusion that this is my life, my first, I was born unknowing. You have blasted all that permanently for me. I enjoy each spring now with thousands of springs behind it. Your fall, the rock I slew you on by a river in India, your to-dos with Alan in the years between these, of which I know nothing, all this I see when I see your leap on Cornelia Street. But cannot help feeling that

piece of ground is holy. As if the sidewalk itself should
bear some permanent mark.

OCTOBER 27
And so the anniversary of your death dawns clear. The
sunlight you bought last year is with us still. Making
jewels out of everything. The dust motes dance in the
air. We are leaving the hotel, I don't know for where.
I don't know if together, or apart
we are setting out.
You have won this much for us, you have cut us loose
Charles who no longer works, Debbie Lee making
    dances
The children sit on the floor in a patch of sunlight
playing with Halloween pumpkins, they keep saying
    MEOW
 to their Halloween pumpkins.
I have never been so light, the jewel that the sun is
is something I'll wear in my forehead now, your last
    present to me
we have stepped off that edge that I've written about
    for so long
The freedom of walking the gangplank,
or of your leap
"go take a long walk on a short pier"
Alex sits on a coloring book like a magic carpet
He rides it across the room
"Goodbye," he says, "I'm Leaving You Forever"
The stapler is jeweled, two volumes of Paracelsus
the toy box, the back of the chair, my shoulder
Mini wears her mask on the top of her head like a hat
two extra eyes stare at the ceiling
THIS IS THE LIGHT WE WALK IN FROM NOW ON

this freedom like swimming in space, no north, no
   south
your gift, one year in birthing.

Shall I no longer hear your voice in the shop, and wheel,
expecting to see you at my shoulder? Will you no longer
fill my dreams in strange hotels? Have you indeed found
another, diminutive body to use for your ends? Or shall
you be born to me in Nova Scotia, a dark and stormy
sun on the weaving fogs? Whose will do you fly from
now? Goodbye, friend, finally. Spread yourself thin as
the sunshine, tissue-thin, and play, and play, and play.

Memorial to Freddie Herko, by George Herms